What readers are saying…

"Kirin Alolkoy has written a superb account of using IFS to understand and heal the wounds of societal and familial expectations about gender and one's body. Whether you are new to or familiar with IFS and the multidimensional aspects of gender, Kirin offers an inspirational model for exploring and overcoming long-standing inner pain from trauma and gender indoctrination with graceful patience, creativity, respect, and courage. The main theme of having freedom and choice about how we show up in the world is vital for everyone."

—Larry Rosenberg, Psychologist

"Kirin Alolkoy's *Gender Unburdening* is a book for anyone who's ever felt the constraints of gender socialization. In other words, it's for all of us. Yes, she eloquently informs the reader about gender and all of its complexities as well as the wonderfully healing psychological model of Internal Family Systems (IFS). But the book truly comes to life when Kirin shares the dialogues she's had with one particular 'part' regarding the distress it's been carrying as a result of gender-based messages. This is where the magic of IFS leaps off the page, showing the reader that true healing can and does happen."

—Kimberly Daniels, PsyD, Clinical Psychologist, Certified Level 2–Trained IFS Therapist

"With *Gender Unburdening*, Kirin Alolkoy brings something truly new, deeply needed, and beneficial for not only the Internal Family Systems (IFS) and trans and gender-expansive communities, but for all individuals and the culture at large. Alolkoy courageously and vulnerably shares her personal experience of abuse, trauma, and repression caused by gender socialization and the binary construct, along with her beautiful healing journey using the IFS model. Combined with compelling research, historical context, and the intersections of race and other identities, Alolkoy boldly illustrates the ways in which we are all harmed by, and can all benefit from gender liberation and a cultural unburdening of, the gender binary and oppressive social constructs."

—Sundaura Lithman, LCSW, IFS Therapist and Consultant

"Kirin Alolkoy has written a book all of us would benefit from, learning how to be more gender literate with ourselves, our clients and the world. As a person trained in IFS therapy, Kirin wrote a book that helps us explore issues that relate to gender, what we have been conditioned to believe, and how we respond in the world. It shows us all how to be free to be more of who we truly are."

—Kay Gardner, LCPC, IFS Senior Trainer

"In *Gender Unburdening*, Kirin Alolkoy generously offers a personal and professionally informed journey into the intersection between gender and Internal Family Systems (IFS). This is a wonderful resource for others exploring gender and provides examples and insight into parts dialoguing, an invaluable tool for self-exploration of parts of self that need care and attention. It will be an excellent resource. Thank you, Kirin!"

—Heidi J. Dalzell, PsyD, Co-author,
A Clinician's Guide to Gender Identity and Body Image

"In *Gender Unburdening*, Kirin Alolkoy has given us an inspiring and thought-provoking look at gender socialization and how we can find greater freedom through using the Internal Family Systems model. I loved witnessing Kirin's healing process over the course of the book. Not only did it show me new trailheads on my own healing path, it also left me hopeful about a more liberated world."

—Wren Wood, Certified IFS Practitioner and Integral Coach

"In this inspiring account of Kirin's gender journey, we are invited in to witness the tender, patient persistence of her Self energy toward healing the many wounds of gender socialization and policing. We are all inevitably harmed to varying degrees by the rules set out for us within a sociopolitical system that works to uphold faulty notions of gender norms and a gender binary. Kirin illustrates the healing potential for deep listening and support for the parts of all of us who have been wounded or have wounded others, the parts who have powerfully protected, and those who might be ready for deeper connection and help toward positive change, freedom, and release."

—Shannon Collins, MSW/RSW, IFS Certified

GENDER
UNBURDENING

Using Internal Family Systems
to Heal from
Gender Socialization

Kirin Alolkoy

Gender Unburdening:
Using Internal Family Systems to Heal from Gender Socialization

This book recommends activities for wellness but is by no means
a substitute for medical or psychiatric care.

Cover images:
Leatherback turtle by Dawn Witherington, https://drawnbydawn.com/
Background by AureliasDreams/istockphoto.com

Artwork on pages 62 and 79 by Charlie Alolkoy

Quotation on page 33 from *Delusions of Gender: How Our Minds,
Society, and Neurosexism Create Difference*, by Cordelia Fine,
W. W. Norton & Company, 2010, used with permission.

Disclaimer: This book contains information that is my personal opinion
and experience, and that may be remembered differently by other family
members. I make no attempt to represent the perceptions of any of my
family members regarding family dynamics or any other topic. It is not
my intent to harm any family member, and I apologize if any content unintentionally causes harm to anyone. Names have been omitted to protect
the privacy of individuals.

Two Hawks Press
www.twohawkspress.com

ISBN: 978-0-9967305-8-7

*For my paternal grandmother,
Basha Brooker (1881–1956),
who never got to live her truth
or follow her dreams**

and

Leelah Alcorn (1997–2014)†

---

*My paternal grandmother was forced by her father to submit to an arranged marriage because no dowry was expected. Basha was in love with another man but couldn't disobey her father, so she entered into a loveless marriage with a violent man.

†Leelah Alcorn was a transgender teen whose Christian parents forced her to undergo "conversion therapy," a harmful, fraudulent, and sometimes violent attempt to force an individual's gender identity to match their biological sex. Besides not working, it can lead to depression, anxiety, drug use, and suicide. Alcorn ended her life on December 28, 2014, by stepping in front of a truck on an Ohio freeway. Her suicide note included the following: "My death needs to be counted in the number of transgender people who commit suicide this year. I want someone to look at that number and say 'that's fucked up' and fix it. Fix society. Please." See https://www.theguardian.com/world/2015/jan/05/sp-leelah-alcorn-transgender-teen-suicide-conversion-therapy

CONTENTS

PLEASE NOTE: Pertinent comments are included as footnotes on the appropriate pages. Sources are documented in the endnotes and references.

FOREWORD

It doesn't seem all that long ago that I was standing before 650 people as part of the Plenary Panel at the IFS annual conference in Providence, Rhode Island. The year was 2016, and the theme of the conference was "All Parts Are Welcome?" (emphasis on the question mark). You see, a fundamental concept in Internal Family Systems theory is that all parts (subpersonalities) are welcome. Not just some parts—*all* parts. Each of us on that panel was speaking to experiences where all parts of us did not, in fact, have the experience of being welcomed, whether by the larger world, by colleagues in the IFS community, or perhaps at times even by ourselves. Although IFS-trained clinicians and practitioners seem to readily embrace the notion of all parts being welcome, each speaker that day shared experiences where we felt somehow minimized, misunderstood, or dismissed by our well-meaning and progressive colleagues.

How can well-meaning and otherwise trustworthy fellow IFS'ers have parts who did and said things that landed in painful ways for those of us with marginalized identities? If *we* felt wounded by others in this community, albeit often unintentionally, what might that mean for our clients? That panel presentation and the resulting discussions led to the creation of the Diversity/Equity/Inclusion Committee of the IFS Institute, of which I was a founding member and chair for its first six years.

It was an exciting time. We took a look at the IFS Institute, the trainings, and eventually the model itself for where implicit bias might be embedded to an extent that it was not readily visible. We worked to see how the Institute and the trainings could hold conversations around biased beliefs with greater Self leadership. We discovered how parts who hold biased beliefs, both explicitly and implicitly, could be seen as protectors—and that if we could normalize them as a natural part of the human nervous system, we had a better chance of accessing them, which would allow us to unburden the exiles who energize them. And perhaps most importantly, we advised the Institute on how to create a more welcoming experience for trainees with parts who have historically been marginalized in our culture.

It was during this time that I came to understand on a deeper level that if all parts were truly going to be welcomed, each of us would need to do the inner work to access our own biased beliefs. It wasn't necessarily explicit bias that was causing harm—it was the impact of implicitly held biased beliefs and the notion that having parts with biased beliefs would mean something bad about us. This notion leads to parts being disowned and the biased beliefs they hold moving into the unconscious. Parts don't disappear just because we are unaware of them—they inform our behaviors and can show up as, among other things, microaggressions from otherwise well-meaning people, each of which can feel like a small cut to the person on the receiving end. Over time, in the aggregate, these small cuts add up to bigger wounds and have a very real and significant impact on an individual's health and well-being.

All of this work was embraced by the IFS Institute from the top down, and it felt so healing. And then came the pandemic, followed by the more public backlash in the culture against progress. At the time of this writing, D/E/I programs are not only being cut—in some states they're being outlawed. Schools are being prohibited from teaching about racism. School libraries are banning books that feature LGBTQ-related subjects and stories. The word *woke* has become analogous to something terrible. The bright light I saw was once again dimming.

And then along comes Kirin Alolkoy's beautiful and much-needed book about gender socialization. We are reminded how deeply we're all embedded in the prevailing myth of gender as a binary construct and how it leaves so many of us unacknowledged and unaccounted for. I found myself resonating on a deeper level with how limiting this is, not only for people who identify as trans or gender-expansive, but for *all* of us, no matter where we fall on the gender continuum. I wondered what it would be like if more of us could embrace gender with curiosity—as not only occurring on a continuum, but also as potentially not set in stone—and inquire more deeply into the assumptions we've unwittingly acquired about gender and the resulting expectations of ourselves and others.

Kirin's clear and concise explanation of the IFS model and definitions of terms around gender and sexuality are incredibly helpful in setting the stage for the parts work that follows—and this is some of the most exquisite parts work I have ever witnessed. We are invited into Kirin's system to observe as she locates and brings healing to parts injured by gender indoctrination. The work is tender and real, and I came away from it deeply moved.

To circle back to the beginning of this writing, it's clear that the gender binary is an example of beliefs that are absorbed by our parts, often unconsciously, that serve as protectors to the individual system in which they live, but that end up causing harm to other parts of us as well as other people. For those of us who work toward Self-to-Self connection in relationships, it is imperative that we do the work to access these parts in order to witness their stories and eventually help them unburden their limiting beliefs. IFS gives us the tools to do this work, and Kirin's book gives us an inspiring example of what it can look like.

As Kirin shares her journey with us in all of its beautiful vulnerability, we see the benefit of not only personal unburdening for parts wounded by gender indoctrination, but also the possibilities of a cultural unburdening, where each of us could be freer to step more fully into who we truly are. I, for one, am more fully awakened for having witnessed it.

—Kate Lingren, LICSW, Certified IFS Therapist; faculty member, Boston College School of Social Work; founding member and former chair of the IFS Institute's D/E/I Committee

INTRODUCTION

Gender socialization has fascinated me ever since I was an undergraduate student in the early 1970s. I attended Oakland University, in Michigan, and was fortunate to take quite a few classes from Dr. Judith K. Brown, a cultural anthropologist who introduced me to the fields of gender studies and cross-cultural analysis. I vividly remember a class she co-taught with a sociologist titled Sex Roles in Cross-Cultural Perspective. My class project involved watching hours of children's cartoons every day for a month and carefully documenting the gender-based messages being conveyed through the characters. *The Flintstones* seemed particularly fraught with gender stereotypes, but really they all were, and so was every non-cartoon show I can remember from that time. Television seemed to be trying to ram traditional gender roles down everyone's throats, and so did the rest of the world.

Long before I had language for gender socialization and started to understand it as a form of indoctrination, I was pushing back against it. Gender-based dress codes were the norm when I started kindergarten in 1956, and as someone assigned female at birth, I was expected to wear girl-clothes. I wasn't an outspoken child—I'd already developed my go-to strategy of keeping under the radar to try to stay out of the line of fire of my overbearing family—but I refused to go to school unless I could wear pants. I was so adamant in my refusal that my mother called the principal the night before the first day of class to request permission for me to disregard the dress code. I showed up victorious the next morning in my favorite clothes: soft gray flannel pants and a gray-and-pink flannel shirt. My outfit did little to ease my anxiety about the big, scary world, but it did establish that my relationship with it would be at least partially on my terms.

During my childhood, my mother was somewhat less locked into traditional gender roles than many of her contemporaries, but the pressures to conform intensified during the years leading up to puberty. She was intent on teaching me domestic skills, including how to do laundry, change sheets, iron pillowcases (I can't imagine why) and my father's hankies, and more. She tried to teach me how to cook, but that didn't go so well. Cooking became a focus of my rebellion against traditional female roles, and I avoid it whenever possible to this day.

Along with attempting to teach me domestic skills, my mother tried to impart a lot of information about (cue ominous music) Preparing for Womanhood. Here's how it went: Wear tasteful clothes, take care of your appearance, look "put together." Sit up straight. Keep your legs together. Style your hair in a flattering way meant to make you look "pretty." Keep your fingernails clean and trimmed. And for god's sake, start mastering the myriad skills you'll need when (not if) you become a mother. She started bombarding me with instructions about motherhood long before I'd need them, if in fact I ever would. (I didn't.) As a result, my prepubescent years were a massive preview of what my life would be like as a woman—plus, I had her as a living, breathing example. I knew for certain I wanted no part of it, though I didn't rationally understand why. I spent several years before puberty pleading daily with my body not to change. I wanted to remain a gender-free kid; being forced to become a woman—by my body, my family, society—felt like a death sentence. When my body started changing despite my pleas, I felt terrified and betrayed, and I declared war on it.

Over the years, my war on my disloyal body morphed into a tight knot of interwoven distresses. In addition to feeling profoundly betrayed, I hated living in a female body, hated the gender-based expectations placed on me (even if I didn't comply), hated the endless uninvited comments about my body ("You'd be so pretty if you just lost weight"), hated the fact that everyone known and unknown seemed to parrot the same messages. That knot also included complete alienation from my own body—honestly, I didn't want anything to do with it. I didn't want anything to do with other people's bodies, either. I became touch-phobic and isolated myself from people as much as I could. Other people had betrayed me by not supporting me and by trying to turn me into someone I wasn't. Although my basic needs for regular meals and a place to sleep were met, my emotional needs weren't even on my parents' radar. I was furious with the world and had no place to turn.

I did encounter a few life preservers along the way. I credit a huge chestnut horse named Boomer with keeping me alive when I was a teen. I'm fairly certain I would have ended my life if not for his help in connecting me with my life force. Another life preserver came from a professor at the University of Colorado–Boulder who helped me connect some dots about the intersection of power and gender during a summer institute on feminism in 1975. Therapy—particularly Internal Family Systems (IFS)—strengthened my trust in myself and my determination to follow my own path. And I finally found a kindred spirit when I met Charlie, my beloved, at age fifty-eight.

Even so, I was well into my sixties before I got some specific help for the knot of distresses I'd carried since puberty. The concept of gender was being deconstructed in the culture around me, and some things had started to click. I grew up trusting my internal sense of revulsion about gender socialization but without a name for my type of person. Was I a tomboy? A lesbian? A freak? None of the categories felt like a good fit until I came across the word *agender* several years ago. It's a subset of *nonbinary*, which is often understood to mean having an internal sense of being both a man and a woman. I have no sense of either.

I'd been working with an IFS therapist on several different issues, and at some point the trails we'd been following kept leading toward how traumatic puberty was for me. That therapist had no training or experience in working with gender-related concerns, which prompted me to seek out an IFS therapist who did. At the time, I decided to continue to work with the first therapist, but I had several consultations with the second— Sundaura Lithman, LCSW. Those few conversations provided me with enough of an inkling of how to start to loosen the knot and hopefully heal it. It feels as though I've now healed the essence of the gender piece. The process by which I reached that point is documented in Chapter 4.

———

I have several reasons for writing this book. First, I hope to provide IFS therapists and practitioners with a useful window into how parts (subpersonalities) negatively impacted by gender socialization might present and might want, and benefit from, support from Self. In sharing dialogues with my parts, I invite IFS professionals to be "flies on the wall" of my inner process. There aren't currently a lot of IFS resources on gender, and I've received encouragement from several IFS folks to contribute to the field.*

Second, I hope this book can be useful to IFS clients as well as others who feel drawn to use IFS to work independently with their parts who have been negatively impacted by gender socialization. It's been incredibly liberating to have a safe place for my own parts to express their truths and needs. I hope my experiences can help others find similar relief from the toxic soup of gender-based messages we all swim in, regardless of how they identify with regard to their gender.

Finally, I'm writing this book because I believe I have a unique perspective to offer as an agender person who's known all my life and who went through puberty long before gender-affirming care was available. I didn't have the option of delaying puberty with hormone blockers, nor of reaching adulthood in a neutral body, as I'd dreamed of being able to do. As an adult, I've had too many surgeries to choose to undergo more, though none exist that could make my body as androgynous as I'd like. As a result, I've had to find other ways to make peace with the legacy of having been born in a body that doesn't match my gender identity. It's been a long and difficult journey to get here, but thankfully, I have.

With that said, I want to clarify that this book isn't primarily about being agender or healing from gender dysphoria—the main focus is healing the impact of gender socialization on our parts. This impact shows up differently in different people and parts, of course. Since I use myself and my parts as the subject

---

*An excellent resource for IFS professionals is "Embodying IFS with Trans and/or Nonbinary Communities: All Genders Welcome," by Sand Chang, in *Altogether Us: Integrating the IFS Model with Key Modalities, Communities, and Trends*, edited by Jenna Riemersma.

of an extended written "demo," I share how my experience of gender socialization resulted in gender dysphoria as well as anger, hopelessness, and overwhelm about being pressured to conform to traditional female norms. Those facets of my personal history were compounded by other aspects of my childhood, including abuse and neglect.

A different author could have written a book with the same main theme but a different "subplot"—perhaps being exposed to debilitating pressure to join the military to get "toughened up" or being forcibly immersed in diet culture and the world of beauty pageants. Or, as was true of my grandmother, having to submit to an arranged marriage.

People and their parts have been harmed by gender socialization in myriad ways, and the extent to which their mental health has suffered and their potential restricted varies widely. Although some of my parts were injured by those types of treatment, I internalized gender-based prescriptions less than most people and, over time, became less and less interested in participating in them at all. The alternatives offered by the gender binary simply don't speak to me, and I have no internal frame of reference for them, which is why I identify as agender. If your gender *does* align with societal standards, this book can help you understand how to support other people well, and you may also find it useful to explore how those standards impacted your parts. And regardless of gender identity, *all* readers (and parts) who feel limited, trapped, or oppressed by those standards may find it reassuring to know there's more support as well as cultural understanding than there used to be—and more paths to healing the harm done.

Regardless of my gender identity, my experience of healing from gender socialization was shaped in significant ways by having been assigned female at birth, and others assigned female at birth, regardless of how they identify, will likely resonate with many of the concerns my parts express in Chapter 4. If I'd been assigned male at birth, my healing journey would have been notably different and would likely have been riddled with pressures to be competitive, suppress my emotions, and "take it like a man." I can't speak for those people,* but the IFS process can no doubt be effective for them as well. *Everyone* raised in a patriarchal society has been significantly shaped by gender socialization, and our systems likely all took on emotional burdens that IFS can be powerfully effective in healing.

Every individual will have a different path to healing, and people with strong shaming and guilting parts will have an added layer to heal† that's not included in this book since it's not a significant aspect of my internal system. (Catastrophizing parts are much more relevant to my system.) My experience is by no means intended to be an exhaustive exploration of gender-focused IFS healing. Rather, it's meant to serve as an example to help illuminate some gender-related burdens and how to release them using IFS.

The main content of this book consists of:
- **Chapter 1: Internal Family Systems** – If you're an IFS therapist or practitioner or someone else already well versed in IFS, feel free to skip this chapter.
- **Chapter 2: Gender** – Even if you're already gender-informed, you may find this chapter useful to get a sense of where I'm

---

*See *He/She/They* by transgender educator Schuyler Bailar for insightful reflections on gender programming from having walked in the world as both a woman and a man.

†See *Internal Family Systems Therapy for Shame and Guilt* by Martha Sweezy for insights into this topic.

coming from and how I got there. It also includes a discussion of race and sexual identity as two other social hierarchies designed to marginalize. In addition, it provides context for the parts dialogues.

- **Chapter 3: My History** – This chapter provides context for references to my personal experiences in the dialogues.
- **Chapter 4: Parts Dialogues** – Most of the dialogues are with a part I start out referring to as Batman because it first appeared in my inner world dressed like Batman. At one point in the dialogues, this part asks to instead be referred to as Bat-teen. Later on, I call it Henry; the reason is explained at that point in the chapter.

A note about pronouns: While many people in our society think it's disrespectful to use the pronoun "it" for a person, most of my parts prefer it. "They" and "Them" can be confusing to some of my parts, and most of them react to feminine pronouns the same way they reacted to gender socialization when I was young: as an unwelcome layer of garbage that others were imposing on me. My feeling is that if "it" is good enough for whales, puffins, and sea turtles, it's high praise. Also, I honor whatever language my parts prefer. In my everyday life, I'd be happiest avoiding pronouns altogether and simply be referred to as Kirin, but I also use "she" and "her"—not because they fit but because I haven't come up with anything that feels better to my system.

A bit of background about me is relevant here to set the stage for what follows. I've been fascinated with the workings of people's inner worlds since I first saw a therapist at age nineteen. Ever since then, the guiding question in my life has been *How do people heal and grow?* I've been a licensed professional mental health counselor since 1996, and although I no longer work in that capacity, my training and experience as a therapist continue to inform my understanding of how people heal. I earned my first coaching certification in 2007 and have earned several others since, including the designation Board Certified Coach in 2011. I've been part of the IFS community since my Level 1 training in 2007–2008. I've since completed Levels 2 and 3 (2008–2009) as well as many IFS workshops and other programs. IFS has been a huge part of my professional life as a certified life and purpose coach, and I've also explored personal concerns with various IFS therapists. In addition, I've copyedited several books by IFS founder Dick Schwartz as well as books by several other IFS therapists.

I share this information not to boast but rather as a way to say that my trainings and experience with IFS—as both a practitioner and client as well as someone who uses it daily in my personal life—have given me the confidence to regularly work with some of my parts on my own. In fact, I began dialoguing with my parts long before I ever heard of IFS. In 1989, I attended a weeklong workshop with the late psychology professor and art therapist Nina Menrath, who taught for many years at Sonoma State University. When some difficult feelings arose during a workshop session, she recommended dialoguing with them. Her suggestion opened the door to a new relationship with my inner world. Over the years, this dialoguing process, which incorporated both words and art, helped me calm down and make noticeable progress in healing distressed parts. I'd used this approach fairly regularly for more than fifteen years by the time IFS entered my life.

Adding IFS to the mix took my parts dialogues to an entirely new level. I've experienced some startling breakthroughs over the years by dialoguing with parts, but none as dramatic as the ones about gender that are documented in this book. The key to my success around gender originated in finally, with the help of an IFS therapist, being able to identify distinct threads in the knot of distresses I'd been living with since puberty. Beyond that, the genius of the basic IFS process—unblending, befriending, witnessing, updating, do-over, retrieval, unburdening, inviting in positive qualities, and integration—was key. As is evident in the dialogues, this process happened organically rather than sequentially, with various components arising out of order and revisited multiple times. My job was to stay present, follow the process, and regain Self leadership when another part came up.

To be clear, not everyone who has gender-based distress will have sufficient experience with IFS and access to Self to do this work on their own. I strongly encourage readers who do not to find a supportive, gender-informed IFS professional. I also want to clarify that I *don't* have the same level of access to Self in certain other areas of my life. That's particularly true regarding the consequences of having cut off from my body due to childhood abuse, gender socialization, puberty, and multiple traumas since then. I continue to work with an IFS professional on that and certain other issues.

At any rate, I've found a much greater sense of peace since opening extended conversations with parts of me impacted by gender socialization, and they're feeling much more connected to me and confident about my support. This work has significantly reduced my sense of inner conflict and helped me feel more at home with myself. It's also reinforced something I heard Dick Schwartz say so eloquently many years ago:

"This shit works."

Indeed it does.

CHAPTER 1

INTERNAL FAMILY SYSTEMS

Internal Family Systems (IFS) is a cutting-edge, nonpatholo-gizing, powerfully healing psychological model created by Dr. Richard Schwartz, PhD. Although its roots are in psycho-therapy, IFS is relevant to a wide circle of applications. It is also used throughout the world in coaching, education, business, religion, legal mediation, and more. In addition, it is an ex-traordinary tool for personal growth and for harmonizing inti-mate, family, and community relationships.

The IFS model asserts that clients are naturally whole and creative, and have within them the resources they need, both to heal and to live fulfilling, balanced lives. An IFS therapist or practitioner's essential role is to facilitate the client's access to their inner resources.

IFS recognizes that our psyches are comprised of different as-pects, which IFS refers to as *parts*. Each part has its own perspec-tive, feelings, memories, motivations, and goals. For example, one part might feel drawn to become a public speaker, while another might be terrified of the prospect. We all have a range of parts. Examples include a pusher, a pleaser, a rebel, an aban-doned child, an inner critic, a caretaker, and so on.

IFS also recognizes that each of us has a Self—a spiritual center that is compassionate, resilient, and grounded. Self is the healing force in each of us and the natural leader of our internal system. A key goal in IFS is to restore Self to the leadership role. Healing happens as a result of contact between a part and Self. Ideally, the client's Self is the source of healing, but another person's Self (such as that of a partner or an IFS therapist or practitioner) can also be a source of healing for a person's parts. It's important to note, however, that the goal of IFS work is for the client's Self—not someone else's—to be in the primary role of caring for the client's parts.

The name "Internal Family Systems" is an outgrowth of family systems theory, a branch of therapy first introduced by Dr. Murray Bowen that suggests individuals in a family can't be understood in isolation—they must be considered in the context of their family milieu. This theory holds that a family is an interconnected, interdependent emotional unit and that the dynamics among family members reflect this interconnectedness, not simply the individual nature of each member.

According to family systems theory, a system (family) has a point of equilibrium in which each member is fulfilling their role appropriately, according to relationship agreements. A change in one person's functioning within the system, whether in a healthy or unhealthy direction, will reverberate throughout the system and impact the ways in which other members behave. For example, if a high-functioning father becomes chronically ill and can no longer work, his partner will likely pick up the slack by taking on additional responsibilities, both at work and at home. A teenage daughter, seeing the second parent's distress as a result of the added workload, may step in as a substitute parent in caring for a younger brother. The boy will be impacted by the shifts in his relationships with both parents as well as his sister. New patterns of family dynamics will develop, always in pursuit of equilibrium; however, the patterns may become dysfunctional if certain family members are working too hard and become unable to sustain that level of functioning or if they continue to overfunction at the expense of their mental health or other aspects of their lives.

Internal Family Systems applies the concept of an interconnected, interdependent system to the inner world of an individual. The IFS model suggests that a person's parts interact with each other in ways that are analogous to members of a family. When Self is in the leadership role, a person's parts have confidence in Self's ability to lead, which frees them to assume their natural role within the system instead of having to step forward and take charge, a task for which they are not equipped. However, they will step in if they see a need for someone to take the reins, and they'll come up with the best leadership strategy they can, however ineffective it may be in the long run. Parts' adaptive strategies can persist long after the original need for them occurred. IFS offers tools for helping parts release strategies that are no longer needed or useful.

Dick Schwartz developed IFS as a result of years of work with therapy clients who described their experiences of their parts, some who were in extreme distress. He noticed that when clients' parts felt safe and their concerns were witnessed and compassionately addressed, they calmed down and willingly consented to the leadership of the client's Self and even welcomed it. Over time, Schwartz fleshed out the IFS model, delineating different types of parts and ways to work with them as well as many other aspects of the model, which continues to evolve.

Assumptions of the IFS Model

- It's the normal state of our mind to be subdivided into parts—what Schwartz refers to as "multiplicity of the mind." Having parts is not a reaction to anything that happens to us, and there's no shame whatsoever in having parts. Normalizing the natural state of multiplicity can create a more spacious environment for bringing curiosity to whatever parts are there, how our unique inner system is set up, and which parts are being triggered at any given time.

- It's also normal to have a Self—*everyone* has a Self. Self is always whole and unharmed. It cannot be damaged, regardless of what happens to us during our lives. Schwartz has identified eight C words that describe qualities of the Self:

    calmness   curiosity   clarity   compassion
    confidence   creativity   courage   connectedness

  Other IFS folks add *choice* and *community/collectivism*.

- We're born with our parts either manifest or in potential, as well as with a Self.

- Each of our parts has an important positive function in our inner system. IFS refers to this positive function as the part's *preferred role*. When parts are in their preferred roles, they are in balance and are not in distress. They're functioning in a healthy way and are able to make their full contribution to our inner system.

- Self is meant to be the natural leader of our inner system. If we live in a safe enough environment, this will happen naturally—our parts will be able to stay in their preferred roles, and Self will emerge as the natural leader of the system.

However, if we're parented by people who are more parts-led than Self-led, our parts will pick up false beliefs and painful emotions as a result of how our parents (and other people) are relating to us. These beliefs and emotions constrain parts by causing suffering and by limiting their outlook on what's possible in life. IFS refers to these false beliefs and painful emotions as *burdens*. Examples of false beliefs include:

— I'm not lovable.

— I'm only lovable if I get straight As, be compliant, play sports, be conventionally attractive, and so on.

— If I don't constantly work hard, I'll fail.

— There's no place for me in the world.

— I'm a bother.

— I'm stupid.

IFS distinguishes several types of burdens:

— *Personal burdens* result from events and situations in our lived experience as individuals.

— *Cultural burdens* are extreme beliefs and emotions that originate in our culture. In the United States, they develop in response to such things as racism, individualism, materialism, and patriarchy.

— *Legacy burdens* are handed down intergenerationally from parents, grandparents, or ancestors.

The parts dialogues in Chapter 4 involve personal and cultural burdens. If distress had persisted after repeated unburdenings, it would have made sense to explore the possibility of legacy burdens being present. IFS has special protocols for healing legacy burdens that are outside the scope of this book.

- Parts who carry burdens take on extreme roles due to memories of negative consequences. These parts generally operate as if negative conditions in the past are still in effect. For example, a part who carries memories of being severely punished for speaking up might force a person to be passive and stay quiet, thinking the danger is still present.

- Every part carries *positive intent*. Even when parts manifest in negative, unhealthy, destructive, or otherwise extreme ways, at their core they're always trying to help us. There aren't any bad parts; any parts who are acting in dysfunctional ways are either good parts stuck in bad roles or else they're just scared. The goal of IFS is never to eliminate any parts—the goal is to help each one find its preferred (non-extreme) role so it can express its wisdom and gifts.

  For example, a part who keeps a person hypervigilant is likely attempting to keep them safe from danger. A taskmaster part may drive a person to work all the time in hopes of avoiding judgment from others. A standoffish part may be trying to protect a person from being manipulated or smothered.

- In contrast to psychotherapy approaches that endeavor to instill in clients new skills and resources, IFS is considered a constraint-release model. Self is regarded as our essential nature, and the reason we don't embody it all the time is that parts in distress block it. Healing is about removing those constraints by attending to parts and helping them find their positive, preferred roles.

- In order for Self's healing resources to be available to a person's inner system, Self must be differentiated from parts. When a client is *blended* with a part, Self is obscured. Therefore, a key step in the IFS process is identifying parts who have been triggered and *unblending* from them so Self can be accessed. Contact with Self allows parts to be helped out of their extreme roles.

Key to the IFS process is learning how to regain Self leadership if a part takes over as well as learning how to attend to parts' concerns to give them the care they need and reduce the likelihood of takeovers in the future.

- Some people hold as a goal the ability to "stay in Self" and never have parts triggered. In my opinion, this viewpoint misrepresents IFS and sets an impossibly high bar. It's a fact of life that parts are going to get triggered; I think it's much more useful and realistic to advocate cultivating awareness of when a part has been triggered and learning to unblend and gently return to a state of Self leadership.

- As we develop and move through life, our parts form a complex system of interactions with each other. Among other configurations, parts can become *polarized*—hold opposite perspectives and advocate for opposite approaches. For example, a taskmaster part may be polarized with a part who wants to play more.

IFS has specific ways of working with polarized parts. After befriending each of them, and with both parts' permission, Self facilitates a conversation between the two in which they both have an opportunity to express their concerns. (The part speaking up more vociferously is often the one who gets to speak first. However, it's imperative that the other part get a turn as well.) It may become evident at some point that both parts are advocating for the well-being of the person. Pointing out their shared goal may help the polarized parts soften their extreme positions and better align their intentions and strategies.

The Nature of Parts

- Every part carries a full range of emotions. There aren't, for example, happy parts, sad parts, or angry parts. If a part is exhibiting only a specific type of emotion, it's an indication that the part is in distress and has taken on an extreme role.

- Parts can express in a wide variety of ways, including thoughts, feelings, words, sounds, images, body sensations, physical symptoms, and a felt sense.

- A fundamental concept in IFS is that *all parts are welcome.* IFS recognizes that many parts have been forced into extreme roles precisely because they *haven't* been welcomed at some point in a person's past—rather, they've been shunned, shamed, punished, pathologized, ignored, or otherwise treated poorly. It makes sense, then, that welcoming them and supporting them in telling their stories and expressing what they've never before had permission to express will be healing. (Exiling parts is never a wise strategy because it only makes them more extreme.) In IFS terms, this welcoming is often described as *turning toward a part instead of away from it.* The ability to do so becomes easier with regular practice.

- Although different parts have different needs as far as the specific type of witnessing they would like from Self, certain needs surface fairly consistently across parts:
  — to be heard and acknowledged
  — to be supported, reassured, and loved; in other words, to know they're not alone and that comfort, acknowledgment, and appreciation are available

— to know they have someone to turn to when they're in distress—someone to take on the challenge they're facing so they don't have to do a job they're not equipped to do

— to make a contribution to the system

- There are two primary types of parts. Some parts directly experience wounding and are forced into hiding to avoid additional pain. IFS calls these parts *exiles*. Getting in touch with the emotions that exiles feel can be very uncomfortable because these are the vulnerable parts of us who hold pain from trauma, neglect, and other distressing life experiences. Other parts have been forced into protective roles, either to protect the exiles or to protect the entire system from the pain that the exiles hold. IFS calls these parts *protectors*. There are two types of protectors—*managers* and *firefighters*. However, that distinction is outside the scope of this book.

Basic Steps in the IFS Process

- The first step is to **identify a target part**—a part to focus on. Once a target part is identified, it's important to check with one's inner system to be sure no other parts object to connecting with this part. (If another part objects and won't step aside when respectfully asked to, it becomes the target part and is attended to first.) It's also important to check that a critical mass of Self is present. It's not necessary to be 100 percent in Self to do IFS.

- **Find out** what the target part wants to express, often with questions such as:

— What would you like me to know?

— What concerns would you like to share with me now?

One of these questions will likely elicit information about why the part showed up. Parts are always seeking opportunities to express their truths and share their stories. Being witnessed is healing.

• **Befriend the target part** by responding to it from Self. This is an important piece of building a relationship with the target part and demonstrating that support is available. Befriending is often initiated by letting the target part know its concerns make sense. Parts often respond positively to this support and may relax a bit because they feel heard and affirmed—and because contact with Self is ultimately healing.

However, they may instead be angry that Self wasn't supportive earlier (in the past). In this case, it's important to continue to offer support, for example by saying, *It makes perfect sense that you'd be upset. You've been having to do this alone for a long, long time.* It's crucial to accept whatever the target part is feeling and whatever distance it wants at this point. If that feels difficult, it's a good idea to check to see if another part is present who's trying to rush the befriending process.

• **Witnessing** – Getting to know the target part involves asking questions and responding supportively to feelings and concerns the part shares. This process may continue for a while. The part may also share memories of times in the past when it experienced distress related to its concerns.

At this point in the generic IFS map, the next steps depend to some extent on whether the target part is a protector or an exile. When I dialogue with my own parts, I don't put a lot of effort into distinguishing protectors from exiles. Sometimes it's obvious, but some parts seem to function in both roles at times. I simply let the process unfold organically and do my best to stay present to anything parts want to share and whatever wants to happen next. The "tools" for working with protectors and exiles are always available as needed. As mentioned earlier, they don't need to follow the order below and can be revisited as needed. They include:

- **Updating** – Parts in distress, whether protectors or exiles, took on their distress in response to situations that likely occurred long ago. Oftentimes, those circumstances no longer apply and the original danger is gone, but the parts are still living in the past. It can be extremely useful to ask a part how old it thinks the person is. The part may be operating from an assumption that the person is still four or ten or eighteen. Hearing that the person is now forty or sixty and that, for example, an abusive parent died decades ago and can no longer cause harm can be illuminating for the part and go a long way toward relieving its distress. This information can also spark insights in the part.

- **Do-over** – Once trust has been established between the part and Self through Self's compassionate welcoming and witnessing, parts may express a desire for someone to step in and stop a negative past event from happening. (Self can also offer it as an option.) With the part's permission, a distressing scene from the past can be rewritten with Self in the picture. For example, Self can step in and tell an abusive parent to stop. It can be incredibly healing for a part to finally experience empowered intervention by a wise, Self-led adult. Alternatively, with the part's permission, Self can remove the part from the hurtful scene.

- **Retrieval** – Permanently removing a distressed part from a toxic time or place is another option. Self can ask the part if it would like to be taken out of a painful scene and, if so, where it would like to be taken—perhaps a beautiful place in nature, the person's home, or anywhere else the part desires that represents comfort and safety. It can also be helpful to offer reassurances such as *You're safe now* and *You never, ever have to go back there*. After retrieval, a part may need time to rest and get used to its new surroundings before it's ready for additional healing work.

- **Unburdening** – Once a part is in a safe place and has had an opportunity to tell its story and be witnessed, Self can ask if the part would like to unload its burdens—the painful emotions and false beliefs it took on as a result of having to endure and make sense of distressing situations without support. If the part says yes, Self asks the part how it would like to unload the burdens it's been carrying. The part can release them to wind, water, fire, earth, or anything else that feels right.

For example, the part may want to stand on a high hill and let the wind carry away its burdens or release them into a stream through its toes and let the water take them away. Other options include throwing burdens in a bonfire, burying them in the ground, having an animal or guide extract them and take them away, or any other imaginable possibility.

After unburdening takes place, traumatic memories don't disappear; they remain but without their previous emotional charge. If they still have a charge, more witnessing and unburdening can take place at a later date. It's important to follow the part's lead about whether that needs to happen and, if so, the appropriate time frame.

- **Inviting in positive qualities** – After unburdening takes place, Self can ask the part if it would like to invite positive qualities back in that were lost during the original trauma or other distress. The part may also invite in qualities it never had but wants going forward. For example, a part who believed it was helpless and vulnerable after a traumatic event might invite in power, safety, and protection.

- **Integration** – Parts may want to take on a new role after unburdening or at some other point in their healing. Self can ask a part what it wants to do now or what gifts it carries that it would like to express. These kinds of questions help the part get in touch with its preferred role and begin to settle into it. Parts may also choose new names for themselves at any point in the IFS process—not exclusively after unburdening.

An IFS therapist or practitioner typically has these tools in their tool kit and offers them as appropriate to whatever arises in the moment while doing IFS. On my own, dialoguing with parts requires access to both my Self and my parts. I can do this fairly easily with my main part who comes up around gender (Henry, formerly known as Batman and Bat-teen). I'm sure it has something to do with my internal system's readiness to heal this aspect of my life and the fact that no parts are blocking access to Henry. At this point, it also has to do with having invested a lot of time and energy into cultivating a relationship with Henry and the strong degree of trust we've established over months of regular dialogues. As mentioned in the introduction, I don't have that same level of access to Self in working with some of my other parts on my own. For them, I need the assistance of an IFS professional to help light the way.

CHAPTER 2

GENDER

Gender is a huge topic and a hot one these days. Many books and other resources are being published, and it's on many people's minds. I couldn't possibly do it justice, and many others are better equipped. In addition, a comprehensive discussion of gender isn't the purpose of this book. Even so, I want to provide a brief foundation for readers who may not have much of a knowledge base about gender, particularly IFS therapists and practitioners working with clients who seek a supportive environment in which to share gender-related concerns. In addition, readers wishing to work on their own distress regarding gender may find this chapter useful and validating.

Definitions and Distinctions

Gender, or *gender identity*, is a person's internal sense of identification as a woman, man, both, or neither. Gender is a person's psychological and emotional reality. It's based on socially and culturally established ideas about the sexes.

Sex refers to a person's reproductive and sexual anatomy and physiology. It includes internal and external reproductive organs as well as chromosomes, hormones, and secondary sex characteristics.

Gender assigned at birth is the gender assigned to infants as soon as they're born. That label, which is assigned on the basis of external genitalia, is recorded on their birth certificate. Assigning gender at birth—and basing it on genitalia—reflects the fact that the society we live in conflates sex and gender—and, for the most part, only recognizes two genders. AFAB (assigned female at birth) and AMAB (assigned male at birth) are the only two categories usually assigned at birth. Between 2 and 5 percent of people are born with ambiguous genitalia and are given the label *intersex*. Many of these infants are subjected to surgery (without their consent, obviously) in order to make their genitals conform to those more typical of females or males.

Sexuality, or *sexual identity*, includes one's sexual, romantic, and/or emotional attractions toward other people. Even though gender and sexuality are both included in acronyms such as LGBTQIA+, they are distinctly different, as are gender and sex.

Gender expression refers to the physical and behavioral ways a person publicly presents or expresses their gender identity. It may include hair, clothing, makeup, mannerisms, voice, name, chosen pronouns, and more. Gender expression may vary over time and may or may not match societal expectations based on gender identity. For example, an individual might have a beard and wear a dress or combine makeup, nail polish, and a bright hair color with traditionally masculine clothing.

To recap:

— *Gender:* Your mental and emotional reality and felt sense as it relates to your identification as a woman, man, both, or neither

— *Sex:* Your reproductive and sexual anatomy and physiology

— *Gender assigned at birth:* The gender category in which you were placed at birth on the basis of your genitals

— *Sexual identity:* Who you're romantically, sexually, and/or emotionally attracted to

— *Gender expression:* How you present yourself to others with regard to gender

People use a variety of terms to describe their gender. These include but are not limited to:

— *Cisgender*, or *cis*, describes people whose gender and gender assigned at birth align fully.

— *Transgender*, or *trans*, describes people whose gender does not align fully with cultural expectations based on the gender assigned to them at birth.

— *Nonbinary* is an umbrella term for people whose gender identity doesn't match their culture's current understanding of *woman* or *man*. Some consider nonbinary to be a subset of transgender, but others consider the two to be different. Nonbinary people may be both feminine and masculine—in any combination and/or at different times—or neither. Some people prefer different terms, including *gender nonconforming, gender fluid, gender expansive, genderqueer, agender, neutrois,* and others. *Agender* is the term I feel most at home with, though I'd be fine with someone referring to me using any of the others.

Transition, or *gender affirmation*, includes a variety of actions people may or may not take to affirm their gender identity. These may include gender-affirming surgery, hormone therapy, changing their name or pronouns, and changing their hair, clothes, or other aspects of their appearance. It's important to note that not all transgender people choose to have surgery for a variety of reasons, including personal preference and lack of access.

The phrase *gender binary* refers to a system of classifying people that reflects an underlying assumption that they're all either male or female. This topic is explored in the next section of this chapter.

Gender dysphoria is a sense of discomfort or distress some people feel as a result of a mismatch between their gender identity and their gender assigned at birth. Some experience it as a sense of having been born in the wrong type of body, while for others it was the way their body developed that created the mismatch. I didn't want to live in a female *or* male body—I wanted a neutral body—though it didn't become a significant issue until I approached puberty.

It's important to note that gender dysphoria is not a psychological disorder. Furthermore, it is distinctly different from *body dysmorphia* (also called *body dysmorphic disorder*), which is listed in the *Diagnostic and Statistical Manual of Mental Disorders, Fifth Edition*. Body dysmorphia is characterized by a preoccupation with one or more imagined defects in appearance and clinically significant associated distress. Individuals may have both gender dysphoria and body dysmorphia, but they are not the same and do not necessarily co-occur.

It's also important to bear in mind that gender is not a choice or a phase. People don't *decide* to be transgender or nonbinary. If they make it known, it's because they've decided to *share* about it. Coming out isn't a change in identity—it's a choice to be visible with one's identity that some, but not all, people make. I've never *not* been agender, and I didn't change my gender. I simply didn't have language for it long ago. Over the years, I've increased both my vocabulary and my sense of empowerment about gender. I've also become quite a bit better at shedding the layers of cultural programming as well as the opinions of those who willfully refuse to acknowledge what gender is or its natural diversity.

Trans and nonbinary identities are also not a fad, trend, or craze, and they're not the result of peer pressure. Neither are they exclusively the domain of young people. (I'm in my early seventies.) As noted below, they've been around as long as humans have existed. They're simply more visible these days because more people are finding support to live authentically.

A Deeper Dive into Gender

I've been fascinated with gender identity for decades—particularly since I first heard about gender-affirming surgery in the late 1970s. At the time, I'd never had surgery, but even so, it wasn't hard to imagine what a challenging procedure that type of surgery would be, both physically and psychologically. (I've since had quite a few surgeries and have even more respect for the courage it takes to undergo gender-affirming surgery.) I found myself wondering what gender was and if perhaps the mismatch had more to do with society than the individual—in other words, with trying to force a gender-expansive person to live in a restrictive, culturally defined gender box.

That question has stayed with me in the decades since then, and it's also been part of my own gender journey. I have the luxury of being able to present however I want and stay under most people's radar, a lifelong preference for many reasons. As an agender adult who chooses to dress androgynously, I've rarely gotten feedback about it, and when I have, it's been fairly easy to dismiss without confrontation. But my wonderings have persisted about what gender actually is. I have absolutely no internal frame of reference.

I know what society says gender is, of course. I know all too well the messages that have been force-fed to me and most everyone else in the United States as well as the dominant cultures of other industrialized nations. But that's not what I'm talking about here, and it's not what I've been looking for.

I've been looking for clues about what it means *internally* to feel feminine or masculine—apart from society's messages about what it means. I've been pondering this question for decades and asking people about their sense of gender, and so far I haven't come up with much of anything. The question I've been asking is some form of the following:

How would you describe your internal sense of your gender— apart from how society defines it?

Most cisgender people I've asked have initially been baffled and silent, as if they'd never thought about it before. Then they've mainly said things like "That's a really hard question. I can't put it into words—I just know" or "I don't know, but I never felt it was an issue."

I also asked the question of one transgender person I knew would be comfortable sharing with me,* and she said, in essence, "It's more about wanting to feel comfortable with how I walk in the world." Her response suggested to me that perhaps there's nothing intrinsic about gender—that it may be exclusively about how we interface with other people and society.

(I could do in-depth research on this topic and probably use it as the focus of a PhD dissertation—that's how much it fascinates me. However, furthering my academic education doesn't call to me, so I'm following my curiosity in other ways.)

---

*Schuyler Bailar, author of *He/She/They*, considers it a microaggression to ask transgender people how they know unless they invite the question because it disrespectfully implies that they need to document and defend what they know to be true. Cisgender people are rarely, if ever, asked to substantiate their reality.

The Western world subscribes widely to the belief that humans are divided into two genders: women and men. Furthermore, it sees this belief as a fundamental natural law. However, as many well-researched sources have noted, including Schuyler Bailar's *He/She/They*, the gender binary in fact originated with European colonization, which began in the fifteenth century. The notion that just two genders exist—and that gender is determined by reproductive and sexual anatomy and physiology—is not supported by other cultures around the world. The fact that it has become a dominant paradigm in industrialized nations does not reflect objective truth; rather, it's the result of an aggressive centuries-long campaign of suppression and propaganda regularly enforced by violence.

Other cultures recognize up to five genders and occasionally even more. According to *Indian Country Today*,[1] prior to European contact, Indigenous North American societies acknowledged a minimum of three genders and as many as five. For ease of communication across tribes, LGBTQ Indigenous people adopted the term *Two Spirit* for people who weren't cisgender female or male. These other categories traditionally included Two Spirit female, Two Spirit male, and transgender. In some tribes, parents customarily dressed children in gender-free clothing until they grew old enough to make their own determination about their gender. Within Indigenous societies, Two Spirit people were highly respected, and families considered themselves blessed to have a Two Spirit member. These individuals were viewed as having a special gift in being able to see and understand the world through both female and male perspectives. They were considered highly intelligent, artistic, and compassionate, and they traditionally held honored positions in their societies, including as shamans, mystics, and

Medicine People. These gender-expansive traditions continue in contemporary Native societies.

North America isn't the only part of the world where traditional cultures recognize and honor more than two genders. Anthropologist Sharyn Graham Davies[2] reported in 2001 that on the Indonesian island of Sulawesi, traditional Bugis culture recognizes four genders—*makkunrai* (cisgender women), *oroané* (cisgender men), *calabai* (anatomical males who take on many female roles), and *calalai* (anatomical females who take on many male roles)—as well as the *bissu*, a meta-gender group that includes the other four and necessitates having been born intersex. The bissu serve their community in a priestly capacity.

Africa has a long history of gender diversity as well. Among the West African Dagaaba tribe, for example, Shaman Malidoma Somé[3] reports that gender and sex are not bound together. Gender is considered "purely energetic" and has nothing to do with physical anatomy. The Amhara of Ethiopia recognize people who are mixed gender, and the Mbuti of Central Africa don't assign gender until after a child reaches puberty. The Dogon tribe of Mali worship ancestral spirits who are androgynous and believe the ideal human is also androgynous.

Before colonization, the Incas of South America worshipped a nonbinary god, Chuqui Chinchay, who was served by dual-gendered attendants. Today, some cultures of South America are home to *travesti*—individuals who were assigned male at birth and take on a feminine identity, with or without gender-affirming care.

To take the concept of gender a step further, what do the terms *masculine* and *feminine* even mean? Dictionary definitions reliably include phrases such as "characteristic of men/

women" or "traditionally associated with men/women." And we all know the kinds of qualities that fall under each category:

Masculine	Feminine
Active	Passive
Projective	Receptive
Outward	Inward
Unemotional	Emotional
Knowledgeable	Intuitive
Independent	Dependent
Objective	Subjective
Competitive	Cooperative
Strong	Weak

All of these qualities are true of me at various times and in various situations, and I suspect the same is true of most other people. I see no benefit in quantifying them and coming up with a quotient that purports to indicate gender. I also don't see a benefit in holding up the lists as ideals to which people should aspire and conform, and in fact it's harmful and limiting to do so. The fact that so many people who *do* see a benefit are profiting in myriad ways from the enforcement of traditional gender roles—from a severely skewed division of household and child-rearing tasks to political power, income inequities, corporate glass ceilings, the beauty industry, and more—suggests that the entire concept is questionable. In the words of *Delusions of Gender* author Cordelia Fine, "When a child clings on to a highly desirable toy and claims that his companion 'doesn't want to play with it,' I have found that it is wise to be suspicious."

And on the topic of questionable concepts, here's another one.

A Brief Dive into Race

Concurrent with my interest in gender has been an interest in race. On some level, it goes back to my early years as a child of progressive white activists. In retrospect, my parents had some "do-gooder" attitudes, including a belief that they were on the right side of justice and therefore had nothing more to learn. Even so, I'm grateful that they taught me basic humanitarian values and introduced me to diverse people and cultures.

My education in race took a huge leap forward in 2010, after I met Charlie, my beloved. Charlie is half Indigenous (Island Chumash) and half Japanese. Learning how his life has been shaped in both positive and difficult ways by his heritage has been eye-opening. I've also accelerated my education since George Floyd was murdered by police officers in May 2020. That fall, the IFS Institute's annual conference included several extraordinary workshops on race and intersectionality. They were wake-up calls for me; I repeatedly found myself wondering, *Where have I been all these years? How have I missed this?* I felt like Rip Van Winkle—I'd missed out on years of learning and had a lot of catching up to do. I started reading voraciously and also enrolled in an online certificate program in equity and diversity offered by the University of Minnesota. I've since completed that program and have taken other workshops, and I continue to read and seek out opportunities to learn.

My education on race has also been informed by my work writing K–6 nonfiction for educational publishers. Whenever I write on topics such as the Civil War or the impact of western expansion on Indigenous peoples, I need to make every effort to be historically accurate and step outside my limited perspective as a white person. I do rigorous research using trustworthy resources, including those available on the Southern Poverty Law Center's Learning for Justice website, and I also try to track down expert reviewers, such as a recent one with the Anti-Defamation League who reviewed a reading passage I wrote on the Holocaust. In addition, I often ask Charlie to serve as a litmus test. His input has been invaluable to my ongoing effort to accurately write about topics related to race and bigotry as well as to keep expanding my understanding of how they impact people's lives.

My interest in race also comes from my background in anthropology and vertebrate taxonomy. I used to work in the field of archaeozoology, studying animal bones unearthed from archaeological sites.

In biology, the word *race* refers to a subspecies—a taxonomic category below species. Let's look at species first. A species is a population of organisms that share many traits and can interbreed and produce fertile offspring. Species have two-part Latin names that include the genus and species to which they've been assigned by scientists. Humans, for example, are *Homo sapiens*. Multiple extinct species belonging to the genus *Homo* have also been identified from fossilized remains.[4]

Lions and tigers, as two species in the genus *Panthera*, have been assigned the scientific names *Panthera leo* and *Panthera tigris* respectively. Other members of *Panthera* include leopards (*P. pardus*), jaguars (*P. onca*), and snow leopards (*P. uncia*). Lions and tigers don't have overlapping ranges in the wild, so they lack opportunities to interbreed. Hybrid offspring are occasionally born in captivity, but they are usually sterile, and many die young. A more familiar example of interspecies breeding, and one much more likely to occur, is between horses and donkeys. Their offspring—mules—are sterile.

In the wild, some species of organisms split into subspecies over long periods of time. This is most often due to populations of the same species becoming geographically isolated and losing access to each other as potential mates. As a result of natural selection—differential survival rates of individuals with traits better adapted to their environment—as well as mutations and other factors,[5] these geographically isolated populations start to develop different traits. Over time, they may vary to some degree in their size, shape, color, behavior, and/or other features. While these differences may initially be identified by appearance, they result in genetic variation and are confirmed through DNA testing.

Take tigers, for example. As of July 2024, the International Union for Conservation of Nature (IUCN)* recognized nine subspecies, three of which are extinct.[6] (The rest are endangered.) Genome-wide research published in 2018[7] established that the six living tiger subspecies are genetically distinct and that very little gene flow has occurred between them.

In humans, no such clear genetic distinctions exist. What we refer to as "races" has no biological basis and no genetic evidence to support it. Human DNA is too homogeneous, largely due to widespread migration over many thousands of years and consequent genetic mixing. The lack of geographical isolation precludes the possibility of different subspecies ("races") evolving.

In addition, on what basis would different groups even be sorted? Skin tone has historically been used as a primary means of assigning people to one group or another. However, the notion

---

*The IUCN is "the global authority on the status of the natural world and the measures needed to safeguard it" (from https://www.iucn.org/about-iucn).

that there are just a few categories (black, brown, red, yellow, and white, for example) is flawed. In truth, thousands of human skin tones exist, and mine is far from white. It's actually fairly close to the color of a naked mole rat.

We've known at least as far back as the 1950s that no biological basis for race exists in humans. Extensive research into this topic was conducted by the United Nations Educational, Scientific and Cultural Organization (UNESCO) after World War II in an effort to address what its constitution termed the "social evil" of racism. After input from an international panel of scientists in fields that included anthropology, sociology, psychology, philosophy, genetics, and biochemistry, UNESCO issued a statement in 1951 that no evidence exists of biological races in humans.[8]

Science also established long ago that human skin tones originated in variations in melanin pigmentation that correspond with differential exposure to the sun's ultraviolet (UV) radiation due to location.[9] Evidence suggests that heavier pigmentation developed more than one million years ago[10] for protection from UV rays as a result of early humans moving from rainforest environments into hot, open areas. This trait developed around the same time that humans lost most of their body hair and developed the ability to stay cool by sweating. The loss of body hair exposed the skin to more UV radiation, which led to a corresponding increase in melanin—built-in sunscreen—which resulted in darker skin tones.

Humans who migrated to places with less sunlight had less need for UV protection and developed lighter skin tones, which gained them an improved capacity for vitamin D production from the sun's rays.[11] (Another factor related to folate, a B vitamin important to pregnancy, also plays a role. This brief discussion is not intended to cover all aspects of this topic. For more in-depth information, please see the endnotes.)

So, how did physical adaptations to differing amounts of sunlight get distorted into the cesspool of racism we're mired in today? The word *race* was used by Europeans in the 1500s,[12] but it wasn't used in the same way we use it today. Back then, *race* meant people connected by kinship or group membership. At some point in the seventeenth century, however, the word came to refer to different ranked categories of people, with whites firmly at the top.

Ranking people by race was used to justify European colonization of the New World and enslavement of both African and Indigenous peoples. It also became firmly entrenched in the foundational beliefs of the United States. After slavery in the United States was abolished, race continued to be used to deny people of color their rights, and it continues today. Race has been the driving force behind Jim Crow, antisemitism, Japanese internment camps, mass incarceration of Black people, anti-Asian hate crimes, anti-immigration policies, housing inequities, voter suppression, and more.

Race as we understand it today is a social construct. It has no basis in biology. It's all about power and control, which are driven by fear.

And now for a third questionable concept…

A Brief Dive into Sexual Identity

It's probably no surprise that sexual identity (lesbian, gay, straight, bisexual, asexual, pansexual, and so on) has also been ranked. Western culture has deemed heterosexuals to be normal and everyone else to be abnormal and inferior—with the attendant denial of rights.

Since humans are animals, many people have looked to the nonhuman animal world for insight into what's "normal." What they've discovered—and the meaning they've made of their discoveries—is illuminating. Sexual behavior in the nonhuman animal world is varied, to say the least. More than 1,500 nonhuman species have been observed engaging in same-sex sexual behavior of every imaginable kind. They include dragonflies, sea stars, snakes, bats, geckos, penguins, walruses, dolphins, giraffes, primates, and many others.[13] That figure would no doubt be quite a bit higher if wild animals weren't so difficult to observe* or determine the sex of—and if more scientists stepped outside their preconceived notions about what they're actually observing.

Scientific observation has long been tainted by bias.[14] In 1906, a naturalist named Edmund Selous attributed same-sex sexual behavior in male shorebirds to "mistaking" other males for females and labeled the behavior "perverted sexuality." As recently as 1986, W. J. Tennent, a butterfly scientist who observed male butterflies trying to get noticed by another male, reported that their behavior was indicative of a "lowering of moral standards" and equated it to human "horrific sexual offenses." Thankfully, scientific bias about same-sex sexual behavior has lessened somewhat since then.

At least until quite recently, same-sex sexual behavior in nonhuman animals has been considered an evolutionary paradox. Scientific inquiries have been deeply influenced by the assumption that this behavior is costly because it doesn't result in

---

*Many animals live in environments that are inaccessible to human observers, including underground and in the Arctic and deep ocean. In addition, many are nocturnal. Even for the more accessible species, observation often involves extraordinarily long periods of waiting for animals to have sex.

reproduction and therefore doesn't contribute to biological fitness—the passing along of DNA to offspring. Research has also been influenced by an assumption that it developed independently in different species. Kamath et al. (2019)[15] put forth the hypothesis that both of these assumptions may be inaccurate.

First, *different*-sex sexual behavior doesn't always lead to reproduction—far from it—and studies have not been conducted to determine how same-sex sexual behavior compares in frequency with other reasons for a lack of offspring. Second, same-sex sexual behavior in the animal kingdom is so widespread that it warrants looking for a common ancestor rather than assuming this trait developed independently in individual species, but this has not been done. Kamath et al. suggest that the reason may be a bias about same-sex sexual behavior being abnormal. They submit that sexual behaviors occur along a spectrum that includes a vast range of variation.

In addition, reproduction is just one of several reasons that animals—both human and nonhuman—engage in sexual behavior. Other reasons may include bonding, conflict reduction, and access to resources. And pleasure, plain and simple.[16]

Another reason for underreporting same-sex sexual behavior in animals was announced in the scientific journal *PLOS ONE* just weeks before this book was published. Anderson et al. (2024)[17] surveyed expert mammologists, wildlife biologists, and ecologists to determine whether they observed same-sex sexual behavior more frequently than they published about it. Sixty-five respondents reported on fifty-two species, all mammals. Species were predominantly primates but also included orcas, collared peccaries, banded mongeese, South American coatis, lions, two kinds of elephants, and three kinds of rodents.

The survey results confirmed significant underreporting of

same-sex sexual behavior in animals. (Identifying as LGBTQ+ and sociopolitical factors at universities and field sites were ruled out as factors.) Anderson et al. concluded that underreporting was primarily due to the perception that same-sex sexual behavior in animals is extremely rare (a self-replicating fallacy) and therefore hard to study systematically. This behavior is actually natural and widespread among animals.[18]

Can nonhuman animal behavioral patterns be applied to humans? Maybe, particularly when it comes to other primates. Humans are subject to cultural forces that we presume to be absent in other animals, so this may not be the whole picture. But it's no doubt part of it—and certainly another reason to make every effort to get our heteronormative biases out of the way. Common sense suggests that a large enough percentage of the human population needs to reproduce in order for our species to continue, but we have zero worries on that front.[19] And reproducing doesn't mandate heterosexuality.

A Binary Lens

Western culture has put a tremendous amount of effort into promoting a binary lens with regard to gender as well as race and sexual identity. Many facets of our culture conspire to promote the view that there are two mutually exclusive categories rather than a spectrum: men/women, white/nonwhite, straight/not straight. These rigid categories are then quickly and facilely interpreted as better or worse—and therefore more or less deserving of rights, freedoms, and opportunities.

When it comes to gender, many scientists have invested a great deal of time, labor, and money into trying to establish a biological basis for differences—and using their results to justify inequitable treatment of women. Cordelia Fine's *Delusions of*

Gender and Michael Kimmel's *The Gendered Society*, both exceptional resources, document an abundance of studies in which scientific research has been used to this end. A striking number of these studies are notable for their faulty designs, biased investigation, and shoddy interpretations. Even so, their conclusions have infiltrated both popular culture and the scientific world and have been used to justify privileged treatment for men.

Similarly, Western culture has imposed a better/worse lens on people with regard to race and sexual identity—and tried to justify inequitable treatment with pseudoscience. (Phrenology, anyone?) The underlying focus of all three seems to be who has power and how they can keep it.

My purpose in including this discussion in the book is to shine a light on the extent to which distress and wounding about gender, as well as race and sexual identity, aren't exclusively personal. Naming and understanding the cultural and historical roots and the power structures related to binary thinking can help us heal parts impacted by them.

My father used to quote a Yiddish saying that is relevant here: "If a worm lives in horseradish long enough, he'll think it's sweet." We're steeped in horseradish, and in order to get out, it's crucial to correctly locate the source of the dysfunction *outside* of us—in the system we've been raised in and navigate every day—rather than *inside* of us in any flaws that parts of us may perceive. The support of Self, whether one's own or that of a trusted ally, can go a long way toward reinforcing this understanding and can also bring tools to the healing process. IFS is an excellent approach for rooting out the origins of binary-based distresses and fertilizing people's internal systems with facts and support, with lasting benefits. The IFS-informed parts dialogues in Chapter 4 are a clear demonstration.

CHAPTER 3

MY HISTORY

As mentioned in the introduction, this chapter is included so the reader will have a frame of reference for understanding my personal experiences in the parts dialogues that follow. The content of this chapter focuses more on my mother than my father for two reasons. First, my father was available to engage in a repair process with me,* and our relationship essentially feels healed. My mother, in contrast, was unwilling, or at least psychologically unavailable, to engage in repair, so I've had to work to seek resolution on my own. That work continues.

Second, my mother had a much more significant role in gender socialization aimed at me than did my father, so my parts were more directly impacted by her gender-based beliefs and treatment. At the same time, my parts were strongly impacted by both of my parents when it came to various other forms of abuse, both covert and explicit, as well as emotional neglect. Those themes also figure prominently in the parts dialogues in Chapter 4.

---

*Most, though not all, of that repair took place through inner conversations with my father after his death, but that distinction isn't important to my parts. The process of healing that relationship is detailed in my 2015 memoir, *Losing and Finding My Father* (published under my previous name).

Family History

I'm the fourth of five children in a blended family. My two older sisters are from my father's first marriage, to a woman who died at age twenty-nine of a heart condition. My brother, younger sister, and I are from my father's second marriage. I was born in a small town in northwestern Ohio; we lived on the outskirts of town on a half-acre lot with a field and creek behind the house and a neighbor's horse pasture across the road. We moved to a suburb of Cleveland when I was almost nine, to a neighborhood with houses the width of a driveway apart.

My father grew up poor and didn't finish high school until he was in his fifties. (He earned a diploma because one of my older sisters was finishing high school, and he wanted to reinforce the value of education to us kids.) He worked in the meat business for most of my life, including as the general manager of a slaughterhouse, a salesman, a vice president of a supermarket chain in the Cleveland area, and a food broker.

My mother grew up in a middle-class home and earned a master's degree in history. Right after World War II, she worked as an economist for the United Nations in the former Yugoslavia and later worked in New York City and Washington, DC. After my parents married in 1949, my mother worked full-time at home caring for the two children from my father's first marriage and before long three more. When we moved to Cleveland in 1960, she worked from home for a dictionary company, reading books and finding new word usages. After my two older sisters moved out, she worked for Cleveland's Head Start program.

Both of my parents were progressive thinkers, but their intellectual understanding of what fosters a just, peaceful world far outpaced their emotional literacy. We children were introduced to people of diverse racial, ethnic, and economic backgrounds, and many stayed in our home, both family friends and social workers from around the world who attended an annual training institute in Cleveland. We were surrounded by intellectuals and activists, and my parents were both involved in progressive causes that included the civil rights movement, the anti-nuclear movement, and a domestic violence shelter. Music and art were also important pieces of the culture in which we were raised. My parents' close friends included activists, classical musicians, and visual artists.

Concurrently, the emotional climate at home was deeply dysfunctional. According to my mother, my father had been "the boss" in his first marriage, and even though he entered his second marriage seeking more of a partnership, the relationship presented many challenges. My parents both had strong personalities, and their bond, though deep, was also fiery and included frequent power struggles. To the best of my recollection, they didn't overtly fight in the presence of us children, but both were quick to take offense, and anger simmered much of the time.

Their parenting styles were polar opposite in many ways. My father, whose own father was cruel and violent, was an authoritarian tyrant whose anger and nonnegotiable edicts were regular features in our home. Occasionally his rage erupted in violence—hitting, shoving, and one incident of whipping me with a belt—but his steely glares, tense body, and hair-trigger temper became increasingly effective at keeping us kids in line. He was never violent toward my mother or two older sisters, as far as I know—just my brother, younger sister, and me.

My mother appeared to be the opposite, but the difference wasn't nearly as great as it looked on the surface. She believed in what she called "peaceful parenting" and mostly refrained from

physical punishment or displays of anger—with one notewor-
thy exception: she was physically abusive toward one of my
older sisters.

Targeted

I was out of the line of fire of my mother's physical abuse, but
I experienced her as extremely controlling. She was certain she
knew the correct way to dress, act, speak, behave, and believe,
and she had plenty of couched ways of making her opinions
known—to me, at least. She may have had a larger investment
in my following in her footsteps than my siblings because I
was her first biological daughter. My two older sisters weren't
raised by my mother from birth, and my brother, just over a
year older than me, was expected to follow my father's lead
rather than hers. I imagine that when I was born, my mother
thought to herself, *This one's for me.* What exactly that entailed
is unclear, but I grew up aware that she was far too invested
in my decisions. I also suspect she thought *This one's for me*
because that's exactly what I said to myself when I was four
and my younger sister was born. I felt lost and neglected up
to that point, and I suspect some part of me thought my sister
might help assuage my loneliness. I'm not sure I would have
come up with that sentiment at such a young age if it hadn't
been modeled for me.

Two events in my early childhood no doubt strongly impacted both me and my relationship with my mother. First, I
almost died when I was a week old due to breathing problems.
Tests turned up nothing treatable and no clue as to the cause.
At least in part because of this close call, I was raised as a fragile
child in need of extra care, which dovetailed perfectly with my
mother's overcomforting style and need to be needed.

Second, eight months after I was born, my mother experienced a back problem that she considered a physical manifestation of stress. My brother and I went to stay with our paternal aunt for a month. When our parents came to retrieve us, the story goes, I clung to Aunt Rose and refused to go to my mother's arms. I suspect this event played a foundational role in my tendency to be self-contained. As a child, I had a habit of daydreaming and tuning out during my mother's frequent pontifications at the dinner table. This irked her no end. She always made a point of announcing that I'd "gone away again," as if to shame me into refocusing my attention on her. I just looked down at my plate and kept eating.

One of my most uncomfortable memories of my mother—which comes up in parts dialogues later in the book—is of her forcing her nudity on me. She believed I should learn to be comfortable with my body, and her preferred method of teaching that lesson was to repeatedly trick me into coming in her room after she showered and before she got dressed. I'd be reading a book or working on an art project in my bedroom, oblivious to what she was doing. All of a sudden, she'd call me into her room to discuss something. She was always naked and would talk to me while getting dressed. I vividly remember feeling like a deer in the headlights, trapped and frozen, wanting badly to leave the room but not feeling free to. I didn't have the presence of mind to tell her to stop, either, so it happened time and time again. It's no surprise that it had the opposite effect of what she intended: it compounded my discomfort around women's bodies as well as my own.

(My father also had a messed-up way of delivering that lesson: by pinching us children on the butt. It wasn't sexual or hostile—rather, a playful "gotcha" thing. When I asked him in later years why he pinched us, he said, "I wanted you to grow up comfortable with being touched, to prepare you for healthy adulthood." All it did was condition me to flinch when touched. Coupled with his threats and violence, I definitely didn't grow up comfortable with being touched—quite the reverse.)

Even though my mother was both overtly and covertly abusive, she saw herself as a champion of healthy parenting. Because of my father's fits of rage, she thought of herself as the "good parent" and expressed, more than once, her confusion about the fact that we children seemed to vie for his attention more. I didn't, in fact, view either of my parents as good; it was simply that she was less reactive and therefore more approachable. Rather than perceive her as safe, I regarded her as less unsafe. I don't remember ever feeling safe in my childhood home.

Attachment and Individuation

I have no childhood memories of other people as sources of comfort. My comforts were my stuffed animals,* the creek behind our house, and the horses across the road. I'm an introvert by nature and have also been conditioned by my abusive childhood to seek solitude. In psychological terms, it could be said that I have somewhat of an avoidant attachment style except for with Charlie, though I'm not a big fan of attachment theory when it's used to label people rather than understand parts. I think it can be used to pigeonhole people as having either a "healthy" (secure) or "unhealthy" (anxious, avoidant, or disorganized) attachment style without fully acknowledging that "unhealthy"

---

*I have a wonderful collection of realistic stuffed animals that I often use to externalize my parts and guides. Some I've purchased after that type of animal appeared in an IFS inner journey. Retrieved parts often choose one as a companion.

styles are healthy responses to unhealthy situations—and that those responses can confer upon people certain superpowers. In my case, the fact that I grew up with no expectation of emotional support from my family led me to seek it elsewhere—in nature, my stuffed animals, and myself. As a result, I'm what I consider "securely individuated." I don't give much thought to what other people think of me, which has granted me an exceptional degree of freedom to follow my own path.

Many times in IFS trainings and workshops, I've heard that the rock-bottom human wound is some form of "I'm not good enough." That sentiment doesn't really resonate with my system. I had a huge "aha" when a program assistant in my Level 1 IFS training shared that Hakomi, a body-based therapy, describes two potential core wounds rather than one: "I'm not good enough" and "I'm not welcome here." The second one is me in spades. Unlike most people, I don't have parts telling me there's something wrong with me; rather, I have parts who tell me I live in a hostile, unwelcoming world and need to isolate myself.* As a result, I have a fundamental desire to be left alone most of the time.

I also don't relate to the oft-heard phrase "I just want to make my parents proud." What my parents thought of me has never been a big motivator in my life. My mother used to say that my inner strength was evident even when I was very young, though that never kept her from trying to elevate her importance in my eyes and claim outsized influence on my decisions. She and my father had the power to inflict many of their preferences on me until I left home, but they never carried any credibility in

---

*This is likely at least partly connected to having felt unwelcome since before my birth due to circumstances described in a parts dialogue in Chapter 4. The "not welcome" message took root before the "not good enough" message and became foundational.

my mind. She used to say, "I'm your mother—of course you're going to take on my perspective and try to live up to it." My response: "You wish." As far back as I can remember, I've been individuated from her—an upside of childhood alienation as well as a by-product of my father modeling fierce independence.

Inner Critics Recede

Regarding the "not good enough" message, I had some measure of an inner critic until the late 1980s, when I worked with an extraordinary therapist in San Francisco. I distinctly remember leaving his office one day and walking to my parked car. Something inside felt so different that I had to stop on the sidewalk, take a few deep breaths, and focus my attention to identify what had changed. The negative voice in my head was utterly silent.

The only inner critic who remained after that time was one who told me I had a flawed body and shouldn't ever consider being in a relationship because I wasn't going to be acceptable and would get criticized and shamed. I worked with that part in a demo with an IFS therapist years ago. What unfolded was an exquisite example of the brilliance of the IFS model.

The inner critic was trying to protect me so I'd never get hurt the way I'd been hurt in the past. When the therapist asked about the exile the critic was protecting, I saw a little kid who was running in a panic, like a mouse being hunted. The therapist asked me to see if the kid would show me a memory or an image of what happened to make it feel that way. The part showed me an image of my father going into a rage when I was about six, taking me in his bedroom, pulling down my pants, and whipping me with his belt. The part was tormented by the memory of being the target of someone's rage—feeling totally powerless and unable to get away.

In the demo, we retrieved the part and brought it into the present. When the critic saw that the exile was safe, it turned into a harmless cartoon cutout like Humpty Dumpty. Later on, it became clear that the critic part had been trying, in the best possible way its young mind could come up with, to keep me away from men so I'd be safe and never again be the target of a man's violence. I never heard a peep from that critic again. It has now merged with my inner team of parts who keep me mindful of boundaries.

The experience of being whipped by my father also reinforced my sense of isolation. My mother and siblings mostly pretended it didn't happen in order to avoid facing how frightening and out of control he was. The only one who said anything was my younger sister, who joked for years that the welts on my backside looked like hot dogs. I suspect her humor helped deflect the gravity of the warning those welts represented to her: *Stay in line, or you're next.*

Coping with Puberty

The years leading up to puberty were miserable, to say the least. I knew I'd have to submit to "becoming a woman." My parents claimed it was a cause for celebration, but to me it felt like a slow, steady march to the gallows. One of the ways I coped was by developing an eating disorder. Overeating was a way to literally stuff all the feelings I had no other outlet for—about puberty as well as being raised in an abusive home. It was also something in my life no one else could control—a covert way to retain my sense of agency. In addition, my overeating part figured if I carried extra weight, I'd be better able to repel the attentions of boys as well as doom my mother's efforts to turn me into a "little miss." For the most part, that worked on both fronts, but it drew a different brand of unwanted attention. "You have such a pretty face." "You'd be so pretty if you'd just lose weight." I was disgusted by all the attention placed on my external appearance and the lack of interest in who I was inside. Those experiences reinforced my belief that people were toxic and led me to isolate even more.

The years leading up to puberty also corresponded with moving to Cleveland. The move was precipitated by a fire that destroyed the slaughterhouse where my father worked and his subsequent difficulty finding enough work in the small town where we lived. My parents were excited to partake in Cleveland's rich cultural offerings, but the move was an unwelcome shock for me. The kids in my fourth-grade class were already highly conscious of social status and traditional gender roles, and the pressures to conform were rampant. It was clear from the start that I didn't measure up. I became one of the unpopular kids and a target of bullying throughout my public school years. In addition, I was bullied and scapegoated at home. I felt hurt by the cruel treatment, but it didn't undermine my self-esteem or my clarity about what was true for me. It only made it harder to live in the world.

I survived adolescence largely because my parents purchased a twenty-nine-acre plot of land with another couple when I was fourteen. "The property," as we called it, featured woods, a huge meadow, two rudimentary dwellings, and a river that changed with the seasons. We spent weekends there as well as longer stretches of time every summer, and my parents built a house there after my younger sister left for college. The property gave me back some of what I'd lost in the move to Cleveland: a way to escape my family and immerse myself in the natural world. I explored on my own and also befriended a neighbor my age whose family had a pony and a burro. She taught me how to ride, and I was so enthralled that my father, also a lover of equines, acquired two horses, which we boarded with my friend's family. Boomer, an enormous retired police horse, became my lifeline. My relationship with him was my first experience of connecting with my body since the onset of puberty as well as my first experience of safety with another being. Before Boomer came into my life, I'd had frequent thoughts about ending my life, most of which ceased thanks to his loving presence. Not only did our time together nourish my soul, but he also gave me hope that my life could get better.

I counted the days until I could leave for college. Besides gaining an incredible foundation in gender and cross-cultural studies, my time there, particularly the first year, focused on overeating, smoking, stealing, and taking drugs. Over the years, I've heard people attribute those types of behaviors to "not knowing right from wrong," and I think that's nonsense. I'd been denied a sense of agency in my life for nearly eighteen years, and it was no surprise that I went overboard when I finally left home. Thankfully, I mostly moved beyond those behaviors long ago (my overeating part is still active at times), and my life wasn't derailed by any of them.

Child-Free by Choice

By the time I graduated from college, I'd given a lot of thought to the future. One thing I knew for sure was that I didn't want kids. Besides being temperamentally unsuited for parenting, it wasn't a future I envisioned for myself or a path to fulfilling my dreams. I searched for seven years for a doctor willing to perform a tubal ligation and repeatedly bumped up against archaic views of women. Several doctors told me I wasn't equipped to make that decision, and one actually said, "You could walk out of here today, meet Mr. Right, and want to have his children." Apparently he'd never met a woman whose identity wasn't on hold until Prince Charming showed up to mold her malleable desires. I was exasperated to be at the effect of doctors who had the power to say no to a decision that should have been mine alone to make.

I finally found a doctor who agreed to perform the surgery when I was twenty-nine. After examining me and explaining the procedure, he turned to leave the room. Baffled, I asked, "Aren't you going to try to change my mind?" A warm smile spread across his face as he said, "No—it's your choice. You're an adult. I assume you know what you want." In that moment, I felt more respected by a man than I ever had before.

At the time, I was staying with my parents* during a break between projects at my contract archaeology job in New Mexico. If I'd stayed in Las Cruces, I would have gone about my business and not shared my decision with them, but it was impossible to keep it private while staying in their home. When I told my mother, her control tactics were on full display. She kept telling me how great I was with children and what a shame it would be to limit my options. She hounded me so relentlessly to reconsider that I finally said, "Look, I'm having this surgery, and you have two options: you can respect my wishes, or you can keep trying to change my mind and drive a wedge between us." Although I'm sure she continued to disapprove, she kept her opinions to herself from then on.

---

*The main reason I returned to Cleveland during my work break was a new women's clinic that offered reproductive care, including tubal ligations. I knew about the clinic because it was cofounded by an activist friend of the family. I continue to find it ironic that my mother championed the right of women to obtain an abortion but vociferously objected to my decision to get my tubes tied.

When I told my father, he got a furious look on his face and barked, "I think you're making a huge mistake." I replied, "You're entitled to your opinion" and walked away. His feelings on the subject were really none of my concern. My parents had ruled the first seventeen years of my life—the rest were mine.

My decision to get my tubes tied was one of the most pivotal and empowering of my life. Choosing to be child-free broke both literal and symbolic ties to traditional gender roles. It helped me reclaim a sense of agency in my life and freed me to follow creative pursuits that beckoned.

Breaking a Pattern

As an adult, my relationship with my father was no longer based on staying out of the line of fire of his rage and violence. More and more, I felt able to challenge his tyrannical ways. A breakthrough took place in 1987, when the entire family gathered at my parents' house for Thanksgiving. Their dining room was too small to hold all of us for the Thanksgiving meal when in-laws, "outlaws" (unmarried partners of family members), and grandchildren were present, so we set up card tables in the living room. Following a family tradition, we each shared something we were grateful for immediately after the meal. Suddenly, my father snarled, "I want this goddamn mess cleaned up—NOW!"

Everyone froze. Dad was set off again. My initial response was panic, as had been true all my life when terrorized by him. I squinted hard to see through the fog of family patterns to find a new way to respond. Shaking, I took a deep breath, and out of my mouth came the words "Have you ever considered that you can just *ask* for what you want—that you don't have to get angry—that maybe we'd cooperate just because we love you?"

My father fell silent. Self-consciousness replaced rage. After a moment, like an actor who'd just been handed a revised script, he said, "This mess is really bothering me. I'd appreciate if everyone would chip in and get things back in order." We stumbled over how to respond, no more certain of how to act than he. Finally I said, "Sure—we'd be happy to."

My father took leave of us, heading for the bathroom. Perhaps his patriarchal habits created the notion that he was exempt from cleanup. As likely, he just didn't know how to be with us without his anger, familiar as a gun on a cowboy.

No Thanksgiving tables were ever cleaned up faster than ours that year. In fast-forward we whisked plates, glasses, and silverware to the dishwasher, leftovers and salad dressings to the refrigerator, tablecloths and napkins to the hamper. Pots were scrubbed in record time. The card tables were rushed to the garage, folding chairs lined up in the front closet, the dining room table returned to its regular position. A speedy hand sweep of the floor, and our work was finished. We lined up on the couch, breathless, suppressing giggles so Dad wouldn't hear. Emerging lighthearted from the bathroom, he looked around, thanked us, and asked if it was time for pumpkin pie.

I was never again afraid of my father.

My Parents' Deaths

My father died in 1991 at age seventy-four from complications from a staph infection he contracted from an ungloved ambulance medic. The ambulance call was precipitated by heart symptoms that I suspect were related to vascular calcification from having taken high doses of calcium for decades for a medical condition. My father was hospitalized for the last seven weeks of his life—the first week conscious but with a raging staph infection that compromised his brain function, and the other six comatose following open-heart surgery to replace an infected heart valve.

My hard feelings toward him melted as I sat at his hospital bedside. His health crisis brought his vulnerability to the surface and sparked a softening in me. Even as I faced the suffering he was going through and the painful prospect of losing him, I basked in the tender feelings that arose in me. I'd grown up aching for a father who was gentle, and that wish was granted in our last days together.

After my father died, I gave myself plenty of time to grieve and process the emotions that surfaced. I had no preconceived ideas about what form that would take—I simply did my best to follow the trail of my grief and attend to whatever arose. What emerged over time was a complete surprise: a compelling sense of having made peace with my father. I still remember what it was like to have been raised in a climate of fear, control, and violence, and I still carry trauma in my body that needs healing. Even so, the emotional component feels healed. My anger toward him has been replaced by deep, openhearted love and gratitude to have had him for a father. My healing journey is chronicled in *Losing and Finding My Father*, a memoir I published in 2015 (under my previous name). I also purchased a memorial bench in his honor. I go there every year on his birthday and death day to talk with him. I also have a photo of him in my office and talk with him regularly there.

The resolution that emerged after my father died was a powerful demonstration of how deeply people can heal by following the trail of their emotions. That experience gave me hope and courage to dive into my difficult feelings about gender.

My mother lived for nearly thirty years following my father's death; she died in 2019 a few months after turning one hundred. I was estranged from her for the last ten years of her life. We'd previously had more than a decade of tension in our relationship, due in large part to her anxiety and lack of interest in working on it with a therapist. I was unwilling to allow her to manage her anxiety by trying to control me, and I increasingly found I had to distance from her in order to hold that boundary. At some point, she broke her word about something significant, which undermined the trust between us and also had the potential to threaten my career, and she refused to take responsibility or engage in a repair process. As a result, I disconnected from her. Though painful, it was the right decision—a radical act of self-care. Two years before, I'd ended a relationship with an emotionally abusive partner, and I'd become clear that toxic relationships had no place in my life. For related reasons, I also separated from my siblings. My life has become immeasurably calmer, and my parts are totally on board with my decision.

Meeting Charlie

I took a long break from relationships while I processed the difficult romantic breakup. After several years, I started to become interested in being in a relationship again. Working from home, I didn't have many opportunities to meet people, so I joined an online dating site to test the waters. I corresponded briefly with a few men, but I quickly concluded that I wasn't going to meet the right kind of guy on the internet. (At the time, I didn't yet understand that a nonbinary person might be a better match.) In fact, I was so unimpressed with my online experiences that I let go of the idea of finding someone and decided to make peace with my single life. Although I sensed that I'd been preparing for an intimate relationship for many years and felt confident that I'd developed the tools to have a successful one, I had no idea where I was going to find someone who'd be a good match. I knew I'd need to be with someone whose values were far different from those of typical Americans. My number one criterion in a partner, particularly after my previous two relationships, was emotional literacy—a quality I've never seen in an online dating profile. I released the idea of finding someone while also staying open.

A few months later, in February 2010, I had a reading with a gifted psychic. After talking with her about career directions and other topics, I casually asked if she saw me ever having a satisfying intimate relationship. She nodded enthusiastically and said she saw me meeting my "divine right partner" on a walk. Five months later, I was taking my regular morning walk on the side roads near where I lived. Less than a mile into my walk, I saw someone up ahead who was taking photos of birds in a tree. I don't typically get friendly with men I don't know, but being a bird lover, I figured that anyone who was taking pictures of birds had to be okay, so I walked up to him and said, "See anything interesting up there?" We introduced ourselves and started talking as we walked. I knew instantly that Charlie was unlike anyone I'd ever met. He had no pretense, and I felt his authenticity as waves of energy resonating in me. We agreed to become walking buddies and enjoyed a lovely friendship for two months before it turned into more. We got married in 2011.

As mentioned earlier, Charlie is half Indigenous (Island Chumash) and half Japanese. He's also agender* and is clear evidence that people born in a male body don't carry genes

---

*Shared with permission

for male supremacy or toxic masculinity. There's not a shred of either in Charlie. By the time we met, I was no longer willing to struggle with a partner over issues related to gender equality. It's a tremendous blessing to be in an intimate relationship completely free of that strife—as well as to witness his freedom in not carrying those burdens. Charlie is also exceptionally emotionally literate and knows IFS well. We're both mindful of boundaries and give each other plenty of solitude, which neither of us could do without. We both feel extremely fortunate to have created a nourishing life together filled with great comfort and joy. After the challenges we've each lived through, we frequently still need to remind our parts that we live in a safe home with a loving, supportive partner.

CHAPTER 4

PARTS DIALOGUES[*]

Sometime in 2020, I had a session with an IFS therapist in which I was exploring my experience of puberty trauma, and I got in touch with an adolescent part who was mad at the entire world. An image came to me of this part dressed in a Batman costume. It showed up on the far side of the creek behind the house in northwestern Ohio where my family lived until I was almost nine. The creek was a great source of comfort to me as a child; it served as a refuge when family tensions escalated as well as after my father's violent episodes. The part I saw in my IFS session was glaring and seething with anger. It didn't want to speak to me or connect in any way. I decided to temporarily call this part Batman—at least until I could connect with it and see if it wanted a different name.

It felt right to let this part be and not try to press for connection, but I thought about it from time to time and sent compassion and openness to it. Whenever I thought about it, I sent the thought that I didn't want to change it or ask it to give up its anger. I was simply open to hearing about its experience if it ever felt like sharing.

---

*My style of IFS is informed by both my IFS training and my coaching mindset. I work with clients and parts using a combination of classic IFS and coaching strategies designed to spark insight and identify action steps that can promote growth and create new possibilities.

In October 2021, Charlie and I were taking a walk in our neighborhood one morning before sunrise, and we passed a house with huge airblown inflatable Halloween decorations. One was a tree with a scary face and clawlike branches held in a

menacing position. That face and pose resonated with something inside me that wanted to be acknowledged. As I stayed with it, I realized it was my Batman part. Charlie is a digital sculptor, so I asked him to make a 3D model of the angry tree for me. It sits on a shelf in my office as a reminder of Batman's energy and a way to let that part know it's welcome in my world.

In April 2023, I felt prompted to connect more directly with Batman and see if it would be willing to talk with me.

A good part of this chapter consists of dialogues between my Self and Batman (later known as Bat-teen and then Henry), the part of me who declared war on my body. Over time, as I unraveled the knot of distress from puberty, it became less monolithic, and several distinct threads came into view. A brief list may help the reader follow the threads more easily.

1. Lack of choice—about the sex of my body as well as many other things

2. Not feeling at home in a female body—periods, breasts, reproductive capacity, and more

3. Body invasion—being poked and prodded as well as intrusive comments about the size and shape of my body

4. A sense of isolation resulting from profound lack of support as a child

5. Gender indoctrination in general

6. Being bullied and treated in humiliating ways because I didn't fit in

First Contact

April 2, 2023

I went inside and opened a space to connect with Batman if it wanted to.

Me: Hello. I wonder if my Batman part might be available to connect with me.

Batman: (scowling) What do you want?

Me: I've been aware of you glaring at me, and I wonder if you'd be willing to share why you're glaring.

B: I'm mad at the world—the whole fucking world. I don't want to do anything but be angry.

Me: It's fine to be angry. I'm not here to get you to put it away or hide it. May I ask why you're so angry?

I've learned over the years that the Prime Directive in working with my parts is to welcome their anger and whatever boundaries they set. Beyond being a useful IFS guideline in general, it's a crucial stance with my parts since anger and boundaries weren't allowed in my family. My parts are expert at shutting me out if they sense a lack of support and acceptance, and I don't blame them at all. They have zero tolerance for others who claim to be supportive but are really trying to change them (echoes of my parents, especially my mother).

B: Everything worked out wrong. Everything is bad. It's not how I wanted things to be. (sadness)

Me: That sounds painful and sad. Can you tell me about it?

B: Who are *you*?

Me: I'm Kirin—I'm the person who takes care of my family of parts, of which you're one. And I want to say how sorry I am that I couldn't take good care of you when I was younger. I really wish I'd known how to do that back then.

B: So you're showing up now in hopes of making everything okay? That just doesn't cut it.

Me: I can understand how you'd feel that way, and it's fine that you're angry at me. I deserve it for not helping you when you needed it most. It's a terrible thing to desperately need help and not get it.

B: Yeah, it's been overwhelming.

Me: There are ways to dump that pain. I'd like to help you, if you'll let me.

B: You want me to get my hopes up that things could be better? It's safer to stay this way.

Me: Yes, it is safer, and it's completely up to you whether you hold out hope for things to be better. But you don't have to get on board the "hope train" to allow in my support. You can keep feeling *exactly* the way you feel. You'll just be letting me into your world a bit. How does that sound?

B: I guess I can do that. I've been all alone with this stuff for so long. I guess it'd be good to not be so alone with it. (sadness) I've been SO alone for SO long. It's become a way of life to be mad at the world and alone.

Me: That makes perfect sense. It's hard to live with pain when no help is available. It's a very uncomfortable way to live.

B: Yes, it is.

Me: What would you feel comfortable sharing with me? I'm here to listen and give you a safe space to share.

B: I'm SO, SO angry that I ended up with a female body. I never wanted it, I never asked for it, and I was never given a say. I HATE IT!!!!!

Me: I'm so sorry you're having to deal with a body that doesn't feel right for you. I can see how that would be a very hard thing to deal with.

B: Thanks. Just hearing that helps a little. No one ever validated my feelings about that before. Mom used to say I'd get used to it and what a wonderful thing it was to have. Maybe it was for her, but it's definitely not for me. (sadness)

Me: We're here to honor YOUR truths—not hers or anyone else's. Sadly, we live in a culture that has very rigid ideas about gender, and there's not much understanding of the fact that many people don't feel just male or just female. Some people feel some of each, and some don't feel either one. Hardly anyone understood that back in the 1950s and 1960s, and not a lot of people know it now either.

B: You mean I'm not just a freak?

Me: No, not at all! You're a wonderful, gifted variation on the human design. There are many, many different types of people, and you're one of them—a *wonderful* one of them.

B: (tears) You don't know how much I've needed to hear that. I've always thought I was a freak—that there wasn't anyone else even remotely like me. It didn't make me want to change, but it left me feeling so, so alone.

This part had lived for decades with a need for someone to give it an accurate explanation of the world. Hearing "You'll get used to it" over and over from my mother left this part feeling unsupported—neglected, even—and isolated. This last communication from the part also highlights the fact that it didn't carry an "I'm not good enough" burden. Its core wound (and mine) is a sense of not feeling welcome, as discussed in Chapter 3.

Me: I'm so sorry you went through that. It sounds very painful and isolating.

B: I feel a little less balled up in a knot—a little more relaxed.

Me: That's a good thing. What else would you like to share, if anything?

B: I don't want to feel this alone forever.

Me: Well, I'm here now, and I'd like to be available for whatever you need going forward. What*ever* you need.

B: Thank you. You mean I can talk to you about things that concern me?

Me: Yes, absolutely, and I'll make time to connect with you, and I'll support you however you'd like. I know you never had that before. I'm here now.

B: Thank you. So how do I deal with having a body I don't like?

Me: Well, some people who don't like their body have surgery to make it more how they want. Other people find ways to live comfortably in their body. Do you have a sense of what could help you be happier with your body?

B: I feel like I'm fighting my body ALL THE TIME, and it's very uncomfortable. I don't want to be so uncomfortable anymore. I want to feel better. That would help. It's not the only thing, but it would help.

Me: I'd like to ask you a question and see if this is a part of things. Would that be okay?

B: Yes, I guess so.

Me: When you went through puberty and got an adult female body, you declared war on it. Do you remember doing that?

B: Yes, I felt horribly betrayed. I wanted to have a neutral body for my whole life, and I felt betrayed when my body changed. It felt like the thing I wanted more than anything else in the world was taken away from me against my will. I didn't know how to go on after that. I felt destroyed by it.

This was Batman's experience of gender dysphoria.

Me: That makes perfect sense, and I'm deeply sorry you had to go through that.

B: Even now, I don't know how to go on.

Me: Just for starters, I wonder if telling the truth to someone else and being understood helps at all.

B: Yeah, a little. But how do I live with this? I still hate it.

Me: I promise there'll be plenty of time to explore this and share whatever you want to share about it, so if I say something about one aspect of it, it doesn't mean I'm ignoring other aspects of it. I'm just going with my intuition here...

B: Okay.

Me: So, is it better now than when I was younger—when we had periods and had to wear dresses and fancy shoes and makeup and all that?

B: God, yes! That was really awful—and having to deal with birth control and the time when I thought maybe I was pregnant. The thought of having a kid was about the worst thing I could possibly imagine—both the physical process and the death sentence of raising a kid. NO NO NO to having my life derailed that way. That's not what I EVER imagined for my life, and I was furious that others thought I should "leave my options open" or choose motherhood. FUCK, NO!!! NO NO NO NO NO NO NO NO NO

Me: That's right, and I made sure that would never happen. I had an operation to make sure that would never happen.

I'm not so much updating the part since I sense that it already knows I had my tubes tied. This is more about gently showing the part that I've taken action to honor its feelings and wishes, even before we started communicating the way we are now. The part hasn't been alone all the time—I've been an active ally behind the scenes, even though we weren't communicating directly earlier. I'm hoping that will help it feel less alone.

Even today, I know that's one of the best decisions I ever made. You were there, helping me make it, weren't you?

B: That's right, and it was glorious!! It was so important to have a choice in the trajectory of my life—at least about that— SO important.

Me: So what else has helped?

This is an example of a coaching question that can support a part and elicit the part's Self.

B: No more dresses, stockings, shoes with high heels, or make-up. And having a ready comeback when people say we should have had kids. Shutting down those conversations really helps.

Me: I'm glad. And what else *could* help?

Another coaching question…

B: Doing exactly what I want now.

Me: And what do you want?

B: I want to be left alone to follow my own path. I want to be free to live by my values, not anyone else's.

Me: You ARE free to do that. Do you feel free, or are there blocks to feeling that?

B: I still remember what it was like *not* to have that. I need reminders that I'm free now.

Me: That reminds me, do you know that I live with another person now? His name is Charlie. He's also free of those strict ideas about gender, and he's agender, too. He's very supportive and understanding. Do you know about him?

Updating the part seems appropriate here…

B: I've been watching from a distance. It's good to know he's different, too, and that he's supportive.

Me: And I'm going to be legally changing my name in the very near future to Kirin Alolkoy. It's a way of strengthening my bond with Charlie and affirming that he's our family. Those people who stood in the way of us feeling free are gone now—Mom, Dad, and the siblings. They're long gone. I can help you unload any feelings that are left about the coercive, judgmental messages they gave you.

I'm planting a seed about unburdening as an option without rushing it. It's completely up to the part to decide if it wants that and, if so, when.

B: That would be good, but not yet. There's a LOT more to unload, too. I want to do it all at once.

Me: Whatever you want is fine. What else would you like to do now? We'll have unlimited time in the future to talk about whatever you want, but we have a little more time now.

B: I want to lean against you and rest—just rest. I've been through hell, and I want to rest.

Me: That's completely fine. Would you like to rest where you are—with me there with you—or would you like to come into the present?

I'm checking in with the part about retrieval without advocating for any particular outcome.

B: I sort of think I'm already there. When you said all those toxic people are gone, it made me think we're connecting in the present.

Me: Great. Just to make it official, it's now April 2, 2023, and I live in Oro Valley, Arizona, with Charlie. You're absolutely welcome to live with us forever or for as long as you want. This is my room. It's filled with lots of plush animal friends as well as crystals and other wonderful things. *This is your home.* If you want, you can have a special animal friend who's all yours.

B: Henry, the leatherback turtle. He's the one I want.

Me: He's yours!

B: Thank you. This means the world to me.

That's why there's a leatherback on the cover of this book. I named my plush leatherback for Thoreau. I wrote a children's biography about him many years ago for an educational publisher, and I feel a resonance with his ideas. Leatherbacks are highly migratory and may swim more than ten thousand miles a year. They're not afraid to travel far from safe shores, and neither was Thoreau. Sea turtles are a nourishing metaphor for following my own path, and placing a leatherback on the cover is a way to acknowledge this part for its important role in this book. In fact, I consider it my coauthor.

Me: Anything else you'd like for now?

B: (sadness) Can we talk about this body sometime? It's been such a source of pain for so long. I don't know what kind of body I can choose, but I want to be healthier and feel better. Can you help with that?

Me: Yes, I believe I can. We'll explore it together. Let's keep that in mind the next time we connect. I'll check in with you every day and see when we should have an extended talk again. Okay?

B: Okay. Thank you.

Me: Thank *you*. You're brave to trust me. I'm here for you.

Batman and I created a strong foundation for our relationship in this dialogue. The door is now open for future connection. At the same time, it's clear that Batman carries a lot of burdens from puberty resulting from both the physical changes and the lack of support. Batman never had anyone to talk to about its frustrations and fears. That's an incredibly hard way to navigate changes that are both abhorrent and terrifying.

April 3, 2023

I checked in briefly with Batman, and it asked me to call it Bat-teen, at least temporarily. I wasn't feeling well that day or the next, so we didn't have deep dialogues, but I sat with Henry the plush leather-back for a few minutes each day and sent some connecting thoughts.

Early Body Burdens
April 5, 2023

Me: Hi, Bat-teen. Are you there? So sorry I couldn't connect with you yesterday, but I'm here now. I'd love to connect with you if you're interested.

Bat-teen: Yes, I'm here. I'm feeling forlorn.

Me: Do you want to share about it?

B: Yes. I'm so tired of feeling horrible about my body, but I don't know how to feel anything else. I've lived this way for so long. Can you help?

Me: Yes, I can. Thank you for having the courage to talk about this. It sounds very difficult.

B: I don't think I'm courageous—just miserable.

Me: What do you want to share? I'm here for whatever you want to share.

B: When I was very young, I was poked and prodded a lot, and it made me want to withdraw. It feels as though I've been holding myself in a tight ball ever since, and it's exhausting. I think it has a lot to do with why I hurt all the time. I don't like it, and I don't want to live like this anymore.

Bat-teen is referring to the chronic pain and stiffness I experience.

Me: Do you remember when you were poked and prodded? You don't have to relive the experience, but at least an age and maybe who did it…

B: I was born this way. I was manhandled. I was helpless to do anything about it, and no one was there to speak up on my behalf.

Me: Was it from the doctor when you were born?

B: Yes, and others. I can feel my skin shrinking from touch because of it. And then Dad hitting me made things worse, and so many other things.

Me: Does anything like that happen now?

B: Not anymore. You've been good about ending that. But I still remember, and my energy self still shudders.

Very perceptive...

Me: Would you feel comfortable just breathing slowly and steadily along with me?

B: Yes, I guess so.

(breathing together)

Me: This is YOUR body. You have a right to say yes or no to *anything*—anything that feels right or wrong.

B: (crying) Why didn't anyone ever tell me that before?

Me: I'm so sorry they didn't. We grew up in a home with a lot of pain—an *abusive* home—and we didn't get what we needed in a lot of ways. It's awful what happened, but we're not stuck with the hand that life dealt us. We can heal it.

B: How? How how how how how? I REALLY want to heal it.

Me: I can help you unload it if it's time to do that. Or if it's not yet time, I can help you speak the truth about what happened and about the situation. What feels right to you?

B: It feels too big. I just want to lie down and take a nap.

Me: Is that because it feels too big to make a dent in, or is it too hard to take that step, or is it because you need to rest up to have the strength to move forward?

B: Too hard to get hopeful and too hard to make the effort when it weighs so heavily on me.

Me: Thanks for letting me know. You don't have to get hopeful to take that step, even if it feels like the right one. I can help you with making the effort. We can take it in baby steps.

Something I've learned in working with my parts is that asking them to get hopeful can be received as pressure to change. This is likely connected to patterns of interactions with my mother, who was always putting a positive spin on things and exiling painful emotions and truths in the process. Growing up, there wasn't much permission to address problems. Also, my father often told me, "Go to your room until you're ready to put on a happy face."

B: Okay. I feel a profound lack of energy, but I think this needs to happen.

Me: Just check one more time and make sure it's the right time.

B: Okay, I'm ready. What do I do?

Me: Check and see if you remember a specific time when your body stopped being your friend.

B: You don't understand—I was *born* this way.

Me: Say more…

B: I was inside her and already didn't feel welcome.

When my mother found out she was pregnant with me, she was devastated. It was a terrible time in her life—in less than two years, she married my father, acquired two step-daughters, gave birth to my brother, almost died from an allergic reaction to penicillin, lost her mother suddenly to a stroke, and struggled alone weekdays with three young children while my father explored a possible move to a new city. She later made peace with my impending birth and even became enthusiastic, but the impact on my system is undeniable.

Me: See if you can connect with a time *before* then—maybe when you decided that being in a body for this lifetime would be a good thing.

B: I remember really wanting to be here, but she poisoned that.

Me: Then let's get the poison out of you.

B: *You can do that??!!??*

Me: *We* can do that together. Are you ready?

B: Oh, yes!

Me: So, get a sense of when you first noticed the poison. How did you notice it, and how old were you?

B: I was just a month or two growing (an embryo), and something felt really wrong. I'd been in a peaceful state of bliss, just kind of floating and being, and then it was as though some bad energy snuck in. All of a sudden, I felt as though I was being slowly poisoned, but I was trapped, and there wasn't anything I could do about it.

Me: I'm so very sorry that happened to you.

B: Thanks.

Me: Anything else about it that you can remember?

B: I remember wanting to get out, but I couldn't. I had to just lie there and wait, even though I was urgently wanting out.

Me: I imagine that was hard on your developing nervous system—wanting to move and having to suppress that urge.

B: Yes! I'm so glad you understand!

Me: Anything else about that?

B: I got all agitated, even though that doesn't feel like my natural state. I'm afraid of just relaxing, but I also don't know how.

Me: I have two ideas. Please tell me if either of them feels like the right way to proceed, and it's fine if neither one does. One is to collect the poison and release it. The other is to rewrite the scene of you being one or two months growing and give it a different outcome. What do you think?

B: BOTH!!! The second one first, I think.

We never got back to the first one. The second one seems to have made the first one unnecessary.

Me: Okay, great! So just imagine yourself one or two months growing, and get a sense of the moment when you first became aware of the poison. You don't have to make it really vivid—just enough of a sense of it that you can connect viscerally with the desire to get out.

B: Okay, I got it.

Me: Now, if you had gotten out right then, you never would have been born in this lifetime—the pregnancy would have ended in a miscarriage. It's fine if that's what you want, but let's choose consciously. There are other options as well.

B: Like what?

Me: Someone or something could have offered energetic protection so the poison didn't affect you. Or someone or something could have taken the poison out of Mom so it wasn't there at all anymore. Or someone or something could have changed the poison into something beneficial so it helped you instead of hurting you. Lots of options…

B: Okay, now I'm thinking… I want it changed into something beneficial. I really want to be here in this lifetime. I have big stuff to do. I don't want to end things at such an early age.

Even with so much that needs healing, this part has a strong sense of purpose.

Me: Okay, great. So what would you like the poison turned into?

B: Resilience. Vibrant resilience.

Me: Wonderful! So imagine that poison… wait, do you want it changed right before it enters your body, or do you want it changed somehow so it isn't in her either?

B: I don't think I have the right to choose for her—just for myself. I just want it changed before it gets in me.

This part is clearly very wise regarding boundaries. Its wounding around boundaries has made it highly discerning, and not just to protect itself. It grants that same autonomy to others, even if it doesn't like them.

Me: So if it feels right, imagine that you're in her womb, and you're getting nutrients through the umbilical cord. Imagine a clear boundary around all of that in whatever color feels right. You're getting what you need, but it's not coming from her.

An image comes to me of glowing rainbow colors that keep shifting from one to another.

And think of it like a protective field that's always scanning for anything unhealthy and keeping it out.

B: It's doing it! It's keeping it out! It's not just a barrier—it's glowing on the inside—bathing me with healing, protective energy so I stay untouched by her toxic energy. Hurrah! This is great!! *Now I can grow in peace.* Now I'll have a much better chance of living a good, full life!! Thank you so much!!!

Me: You're *very* welcome!! I'm so glad it's working!! So, if it feels right, check and see how your developing body is being affected by the glowing colors.

B: It's blooming like time-lapse images of flowers opening. I like it!!

Me: Take a moment or two to be with that—to take it in.

B: It doesn't matter what I went through—it only matters that I was given the tools to grow and heal beyond it. This is HUGE!!!!!

Me: Check and see if anything else wants to happen today.

B: (kissing my cheek) I'm good for now, but let's do this again before long.

Me: Okay!!! Beautiful work!! You're very courageous—and resilient!!

Puberty Strikes

April 11, 2023

Me: Hi, Bat-teen! I'm wondering if you're available to connect with me again.

Bat-teen: Yes, I'm right here.

Me: Charlie is going to make a "power picture" today of the glowing colors protecting you as you develop. It's going to be really cool!

B: I'm excited! That was a *huge* shift for me. I feel more energized now—like I've shed a layer of protection and caution. Like my life's trajectory is changing.

This is the picture Charlie created. A color version can be viewed at kirinalolkoy.com/embryo.

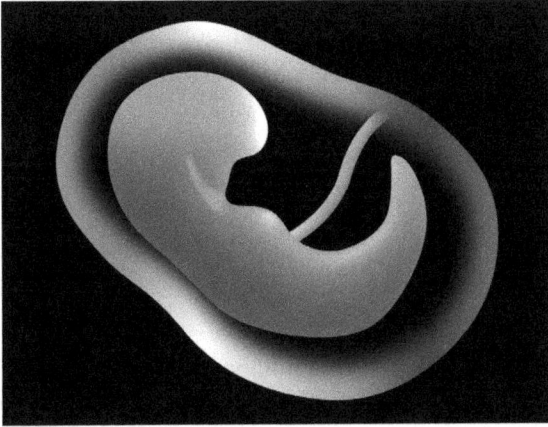

Me: That's great!! How about we change it some more for the better?

B: Yes, that would be great.

Me: When is the next time in your life we should visit?

B: I guess the puberty time, though I HATE HATE HATE it!!! HATE IT!!!!!

Me: Yes, that makes perfect sense. I bet you and I can create something better for you, though.

B: How is that possible? It's like walking the plank or marching to the guillotine—facing doom with no recourse. How can that not be the worst thing ever?

Me: I understand your feelings and want to take time to fully honor them before anything else. Is there anything else you want to say about that time?

B: It was about my body changing, which changed the way people treated me. All of a sudden I was seen as a malleable woman. The gender grooming became even more relentless—to act in certain ways, to keep my legs together, to be "presentable," to think about boys and someday getting married and having kids. I'M NOT A FUCKING LUMP OF CLAY. I'm not a pawn of anyone else's ideas about how people should be and act.

It was also about *no choice*. No one asked me who I wanted to turn into. No one asked, but if they had, I would have said, "Please just leave me alone to be me. I don't want to have an adult body. Let it stay neutral. I like it just fine this way." I feel devastated that it happened against my will. I was forced to have an adult female body, even though I never, ever wanted it.

Even though the emotions are extremely painful, I sensed a measure of relief when Bat-teen expressed them. And even though there isn't a quick fix, simply naming them in the presence of a witness is freeing.

Me: I'm so very sorry that happened to you. Thank you for letting me know. Thank you for helping me understand the truth of your experience.

B: I feel so lost about this. I don't know what can help.

Me: Does talking with me about it help at all?

B: A little. I've been alone with this for so long.

Me: Yes you have. I want to help and support you going forward. I'm here now. And we can put our heads together and figure out what can help.

B: Thank you, but I feel broken.

Me: If it feels okay, check back in with the developing embryo who felt so hopeful and free to develop how it saw fit. Does that feel okay?

B: Yes, so hopeful and free.

Me: You said: "Now I can grow in peace. Now I'll have a much better chance at living a good, full life!! It doesn't matter what I went through—it only matters that I was given the tools to grow and heal beyond it."

B: Yeah, I was very hopeful back then.

Me: When did that change? What event or events interrupted that hope?

It's crucial to connect with the part's life force, not to urge it to push forward toward a good, full life but rather to help the part access the "fuel" for naming what else needs healing. Once those obstacles are removed, the part will have access to its Self and will naturally be freer to create the good, full life it longs for.

B: One was when Mom and Dad told X (sibling) and me about sex. I was laughing because it sounded ridiculous, but I was also thinking, "You've got to be kidding. No way in hell am I going to do that." Then there was this steady march to the assumption that I was going to do it and have babies and devote my life to being a mother. NO FUCKING WAY!! Of all the things I could imagine doing with my life, that definitely wasn't one of them.

Me: May I share something?

B: Sure.

Me: We *didn't* have kids. I made sure that would never happen.

We talked about that in an earlier dialogue, but it helps this part to be reminded that the pressures of gender socialization didn't win. Those pressures didn't stop us from following our path.

B: Thank you for that. You helped save my life. I never would have stood for a life with kids. It would have been better to start fresh in a new life.

Me: I'm curious about the words you used about never standing for a life with kids. What else would you never have stood for?

B: Being shoved around and ruled by Mom and Dad. Being bullied by the siblings. Being poked and prodded and man-handled. Being expected to cater to other people's desires. I'm a person—not a servant. I'm not here to fulfill anyone else's dreams. I have big stuff to do!!!!

Me: Would you like to tell me about that—about what you're here to do? I'd love to hear if you feel like sharing.

A fairly standard component of coaching is eliciting clients' (and parts') vision, which helps provide the "juice" for doing the hard work to make it real.

B: Oh god—so much!!! I want to see the world and connect with other living creatures and talk with them and honor them. I have so much to do in that realm—so much I want to do and that I've been preparing to do for so long. Sooooooo long—many, many lifetimes. I need freedom and space and mental energy to do that. I can't be bothered with taking care of other people, especially not dependent ones. And I can't get distracted by bullshit drama. I just want to be left alone to follow my path.

Me: That sounds great! And do you want Charlie to leave you alone, too?

B: No—maybe not him. He knows how to be here and give me space, which is perfect. He's good support without being intrusive. I never would have thought that existed before he came along.

Me: He's really good at that. Anything else about your path you want to share?

B: I want to be immersed in beauty—the beauty of the natural world as well as the beauty I and others create.

Me: Awesome—sounds great!!

B: And I want to share with others how life looks from my perspective. I know I'm different in a lot of ways, and I want to share about it. Maybe it'll encourage others to be different, too—to listen more closely to who they are deep inside and have the courage to live by it.

Me: Wow—great!!! I support you 100 percent in all those things. Anything I can do to help and support you, you can count on me.

B: Well—you *can* do a few things…

Me: Yes—what things?

B: Don't ask me to get dressed up. I hate hate hate it!!

Me: Yes, that's fine. If we *ever* need to go somewhere where others dress up, which I can't imagine, I'll be sure to check with you to make sure you're happy and that we make decisions together. I won't ignore your preferences—promise!

B: Thanks! That feels good.

Me: What else?

B: Don't sacrifice your needs or preferences for others. Don't be a fucking doormat.

Me: Do I do that?

B: In little ways sometimes. Don't do that.

Me: Thank you for calling that to my attention. I'll do my best to be more mindful. And please feel free to remind me if you see me doing something that's "off." I welcome your input.

B: Thanks.

Me: Anything else?

B: Not right now, but it seems as though you have something on your mind...

Me: Yeah, I do. I have a lot of body challenges, and I think at least some of them come from the time when we went through puberty. I have challenges with my feet, ankles, and knees, and I really took note when you talked about the things you never would have stood for. Language like that can be connected to body symptoms and problems in mysterious ways.

B: Oh—I didn't know that. I'm sorry.

Me: Of course you didn't know. And we grew up in a family that was always "taking a stand" and asserting what they'd never stand for. Can we check in with my feet and see if or how those things are connected?

B: Sure...

The focus shifts to dialoguing with my feet.

Feet: I want to be flippers. I want to go back to the ocean. I'm not meant for walking on hard ground.

Me: Hi, feet! So glad to have an opportunity to talk with you! Thanks for letting me know how you feel.

F: I didn't sign up for this.

Me: I understand that, and I'm sorry you're not happy. I'd like to help you if that would be okay.

F: (forlorn) Okay.

Me: Why do you want to go back to the ocean?

F: I'm just much more at home there.

Me: Yes, I think I understand. Are you a body part or a psychological part?

F: I'm a psychological part. This human body thing is altogether strange.

Me: How did you end up here in a body?

F: I don't know. I just woke up one day and here I was.

Me: What was it like the day you woke up? What did you notice around you?

F: I was all cramped and squished inside a tight space, and I couldn't feel much or grow right. I wanted to get out and swim!

Me: Was that when I was a little embryo inside my mother's womb?

F: Yes! I HATED it in there. I didn't ever want to be planted in that world. I wanted to swim away.

Me: So sorry you went through that. Being trapped sounds awful. I bet it would feel good for you to swim sometimes.

F: I'd like that.

Me: Did you know about the conversation I had with Batteen a few days ago about changing the energy inside the womb—feeding the embryo the energy of vitality and resilience to take the place of any negative energy?

It's been my experience that some parts can listen in on conversations with other parts, but others can't.

F: No. I just know about constriction.

Me: Can I share with you?

F: Okay.

Me: We replaced the negative energy with rainbow-colored energy to create a boundary and also to bathe the embryo in glowing colors and healing light so it could grow into who it's supposed to grow into and have a good life. Charlie—my beloved, who's an artist—created this image for us to look at every day and feel energized by.

F: (looking at the image) That's awesome.

Me: Can you take in, even a little, that there are better options now? It's 2023, and there are better options.

F: Holy cow, it's 2023?! I thought it was the '60s.

Although I've been using IFS for more than fifteen years, I'm always amazed by the healing impact of updating parts. They really are stuck in the past when we first make contact.

Me: A lot of time has passed, and many things have changed. Our original family is gone—dead or thousands of miles away. We're safe now. We can live a gentler life. There's no longer a need to hold tight to opinions or fight for room to be.

F: Wow, that's amazing.

Me: You can relax now. You can be at peace now and live more comfortably. You're welcome to develop stronger muscles to help you move better—and you're also welcome to enjoy the support that's there for you—both the orthotics and emotional support from me (and Charlie).

F: That sounds really good.

Me: Is there anything you'd like to release?

F: I don't want to have to fight for the right to be me anymore. I just want to be me.

Me: That's great, and you have my full support. Do you want to do anything to formally release it?

F: Let it go in the water—let it trail off my toes like watercolors.

Me: Let's spend a few moments picturing that.

F: I want to move like swimming.

Me: I'll find a way for us to do that. Anything more to release?

F: Not for now, but we can do it regularly.

Me: Any qualities you want to take in?

F: Stability. Strength. Power. Resilience. Purpose. Intention. Integrity.

Me: Just take them into your being. They're yours. They belong to you. You don't have to fight for them or take a stand against anything or anyone to have them. *They're yours.*

F: Thank you—this feels great.

It's been my experience that these mini unburdenings can happen at any time—they don't always need to follow other IFS steps in a formulaic way or happen as part of a deep inner journey.

(Later in the day…)

Me to Bat-teen: Do you want to do anything else for today?

B: Yes, I'm rarin' to go…

Me: Great—me too! So, if it's okay with you, I'd like to go back to something I shared earlier today: I have a lot of body challenges, and I think at least some of them come from the time when we went through puberty. I remember very vividly that when my body went through those changes, I declared war on it. I said my body was my enemy, and I declared war on it. Do you remember that?

B: Yes, that was a very, very dark time. I've never felt so alone. It was horrific.

Me: I'm so sorry you went through that alone and didn't have good support. I really want to honor how hard it was to go through that alone and not get help despite trying so hard to.

B: Thank you. It nearly broke me. It *did* break me. I healed some when Boomer came into my life, but I still had a lot of brokenness.

Boomer is the huge chestnut horse I mentioned earlier. He was my lifeline when I was a teenager. My connection with him gave me my first taste of aliveness and kept me from ending my life.

Me: I'm deeply sorry—and so sorry I wasn't able to help you back then.

B: Thank you. I'm still broken.

Me: Can I help?

B: I don't know. I think it's too deeply rooted for anything to make a difference.

Me: I think I have a sense of how deeply rooted it is, though I'm always open to learning more. But I have to say, I feel confident that there's help for it and for you.

B: Don't make me get hopeful. I don't want to open up that wound.

Me: I totally respect your wishes. Would it be okay to ask a few questions about it?

B: (sitting curled up tight) I guess so.

Me: How does it feel to sit in such a tight way?

B: Painful. Everything feels rigid and shut down. I don't like it, but I don't know any other way. I've been this way for so long.

Me: And what if we could help you relax and flow more?

B: I don't even want to think about it.

Me: What are you afraid would happen if you thought about it?

B: I'd wish things could be different, but they can't be.

Me: Well, some things would be harder to change than others, but a *lot* could be different.

B: Yeah, like what?

Me: Like feeling all alone with nowhere to turn for help. And thinking a certain kind of body dooms you to a certain kind of life. And thinking you're the only one who's ever felt this way and the isolation that comes from that.

B: There's a little crack of light that shows up when you say all that. Like maybe it's not a monolith.

This feels significant. Up until now, these issues have mostly felt like a huge, tangled knot. Identifying separate threads is a key step in exploring and healing them.

Me: That's right—and we can address pieces of it, one at a time, and make it smaller. Plus, we're both really smart, so we can put our heads together and come up with some innovative solutions. Also, there's something you should know about me: I'm tenacious. If something looks like an obstacle, I'm going to make every effort to outsmart it. These concerns and wounds of yours are deep, but they're definitely not insurmountable. I have some really solid experience with using

IFS to heal other trauma that once looked insurmountable. It wasn't!!

B: I've never really sensed this before, but I feel a sense of partnership with you. I actually feel as though you may be able to help.

Me: I can, and it's exciting to hear that you sense the possibility. *Building an alliance with Bat-teen feels like a huge breakthrough.*

Rejecting the Gender Binary
April 14, 2023

Me: Hi, Bat-teen. It's me—Kirin. I'd love to visit with you if you're available and interested.

Bat-teen: Hi, Kirin. I've been thinking about what you said, and I'd like to try. I don't like living in such a tight way. I don't mean to cause you misery, and I'm not enjoying this either.

Me: Wow, thanks. I'd *love* to support you and see whether we can both find some relief. Is there any particular place that feels right to start with?

B: Thinking a certain kind of body doomed me to a certain kind of life. That just SUCKED.

Me: Yeah, that's total bullshit. What would you like to share about that?

B: I was sure I didn't want to follow the path Mom took, but I didn't know what I wanted because I didn't have a name for it.

Me: Yes, that's right. A lot more is understood now about the range of options and about how people come in so many varieties. We happen to be one (agender) that wasn't understood back then... but it is now.

B: REALLY???

Me: Yes—definitely. Back when we went through puberty, people thought there were just men and women, and there weren't any options for someone living in a female body besides being a girly girl or a tomboy.

B: Well, tomboy fit me a lot better than the alternative, but I still got all that SHIT shoved at me pretty much nonstop about growing up and getting married, about learning skills I'd need when I got married (cooking, cleaning, raising kids, and so on), and how to set that process in motion by being attractive to boys. FUCK THAT!!! FUCK ALL OF THAT!!!

Me: Yes!! It's total nonsense. But what's *your* truth?

B: It all feels very oppressive to me. I want everyone to stop telling me what I can and can't do and what I should and shouldn't do—BECAUSE OF BODY PARTS!!! That's just ridiculous!!!

Me: Yes, it is. I'm in complete agreement with you.

I'm very sorry, but I'm sleepy and don't have good attention to continue our conversation. Can we continue tomorrow?

B: Yes.

Me: Thank you for understanding. I'll be back tomorrow. Love you!

Going Beneath the Anger
April 15, 2023

Me: Hi, Bat-teen. I'm back now. Would you like to talk some more?

Bat-teen: Yes—love to.

Me: Great! We were talking about how ridiculous it is to assign someone certain roles because of their body parts.

B: Yes, that sucks.

Me: Do you still feel as though parts of you are at the effect of that programming?

B: Well, I'm still angry, so I guess the answer is yes.

Even though Bat-teen carries a lot of distress, I'm impressed by its self-awareness in answering that way.

Me: If it were just about your personal experience, I'd say there's simply something personal in you that needs healing, but this isn't just about you. This is also about an entire system that's been in place for hundreds of years or more that blasts that message nonstop in order to have power over women.

B: I see what you mean.

Me: So I'll let you check and see what in you would like some healing.

B: (checking…) I don't live by any of that, so I don't know… In many ways it feels as though I've left it all behind and am certain that I don't have to go along with it, but I still get angry when I'm exposed to those messages, such as in the news or advice columns. It's such total exploitational bullshit.

Me: Yes it is. Absolutely. Are you clear that you're personally free of it?

B: Yes, I think I am. But I understand that so many others aren't. I'd like to help them if I can. And I have a protector who's ready to snarl if someone shares that perspective.

Me: That's great!! That protector is absolutely welcome here!

When I first learned IFS, it felt useful to try to distinguish between protectors and exiles. It also felt helpful to imagine layers of parts, with protectors on the outside and wounded, vulnerable exiles on the inside. After working with my own parts and those of clients for many years, I no longer find those distinctions as universally useful. Since parts contain parts, and since each of those parts contains parts, it seems futile to get too wrapped up in which protectors are protecting an exile or even whether a part is an exile or a protector. I just go with whatever a part shares, without trying to fit it too perfectly into a map or formula. And I use whatever tools IFS offers without thinking about which kind of part they're designed to be used with. If there's a benefit to using a layered approach to understand a situation, it becomes clear over time.

B: Okay. I guess that piece of the puzzle isn't an issue anymore. Life has changed so much since those messages were transmitted to me. Though I do have some yucky feelings about Mom claiming to be a feminist yet working so hard to indoctrinate me.

Me: Anything else you'd like to share about that?

B: I don't know if I'll ever stop being mad at her for being such a liar and a hypocrite. She was so FAKE. I can't believe she thought she was forward-thinking. She was just like all the others except she was more covert.

Me: Someone said recently that anger keeps us attached to people. Would you feel comfortable sharing what was hurtful without the anger—in other words, getting underneath the anger?

This intuitively felt like a good place to use the layered approach.

B: I can do that as long as you stay with me. I don't want to do this alone. I still feel as though she could come get me if I get vulnerable.

Me: I understand why you'd want to stay protected—and I want to absolutely assure you that she can't get you or harm you in any way. She's been dead for years, and she and I didn't talk for more than ten years before she died.

B: That's great. That's a relief.

It's clear as I work with this part that the cultural taboo against saying anything bad about one's mother is harmful and exiling. Bat-teen needs to be free to say it's relieved that my mother died.

So, I really needed help all along, and I didn't get any. Everything was about shoving me in a box of what others wanted for me, and no one asked me who *I* wanted to become or what kind of life *I* wanted to lead. It was just assumed that I'd turn out a certain way—and that Mom and Dad knew best. But they didn't—they didn't know a thing about me. I wanted to be free to follow my own path. That's all I wanted—but they made me pay the price of doing it utterly alone, and that was devastating. I never had a nourishing family. Even now, I don't know how I survived.

Me: I've helped younger parts than you heal from that isolation, especially Huck (a very young part who used to be stranded alone in Antarctica). But it seems as though you have some experiences to add to the mix—or another layer of isolation that needs healing.

B: I was so alone yet at the same time so smothered and controlled. It's really confusing.

Me: That makes perfect sense. You didn't have the freedom *or* the support you needed.

B: Yes, that's exactly it.

Invasion, abuse, abandonment, and neglect rolled up together…

Me: Do you feel you more need to let something go, let something in, or both?

B: Let me check… Let something in. I think I've already let go of the bullshit they fed me.

Me: I'm noticing these metaphors about nourishment—"the bullshit they fed you" and "having things rammed down your throat." This may not fit, but just check again and see if anything wants out to make room for things that are truly nourishing.

B: That's a good question. I'll check… I want to cough it all up like a hairball.

Me: You can do that. You can release all of it.

B: How?

Me: Imagine a setting where you can release it, such as to air, water, sky, one of the other elements, or anything else.

I got an internal sense of lying on couch with warm blankets on the digestive areas of my body and letting an image come. I saw the part coughing up big, hard masses that looked like kohlrabi (turnip cabbage). There was a lot of turmoil at first, but it became easier. The part coughed them up into a hole in the ground where they'd be broken down. MANY of them came up and out. The process seemed to make room for healthier digestion. I had a sense that the process isn't finished and that more may happen later. I got the impression it would help to drink lots of chamomile tea.

Me: How are you feeling?

B: Better—like I've been through something intense, but I feel better. I need to spend a few days just settling into this change.

It's gonna feel really different to be without all those hard balls of energy/rock inside. Roomier. I can breathe deeper.

Me: That's great!!

It's not time to invite qualities back in. First, there's more to empty out at a later time.

Me: Anything in the way of support you'd like from me now or in the near future?

B: Just be here whenever I want to talk with you. Your support means a *lot*.

Me: You can count on me. I'm here! I love you!

Releasing Lies
April 18, 2023

Me: Hello, Bat-teen. I'm here to check in with you. Is there any kind of support you'd like from me now?

B: How long is this puking going to take? It's tiring.

Me: Yes, I know, and you're hanging in with the process courageously. It's a good thing to get out all the things you were forced to swallow. You don't have to do it all at once if it's too much.

B: I'm ready to stop for now. My insides are getting tired, and the whole thing is pretty disgusting.

Me: Would it be helpful to name anything you got out?

B: Lies, lies, it's all lies. Lies about who I was supposed to become, about what great parents Mom and Dad were, about their expertise on *any* part of my life. It was all lies. But it's out now. Oh yeah, and lies that other people—and society—told me about who I should be. It's gone now.

Me: That's right—you released it, so it's outside of you and gone. The ground broke it down, so it's really gone.

B: That's really great, isn't it?

Me: Yes, amazing. Really great work!!

B: Thank you. Now I'm ready to fill up with truths to replace the lies.

Bat-teen suggested taking in positive qualities, so I went with it, even though the process of unburdening the kohlrabis isn't finished. It's a good example of not needing to complete one IFS step before proceeding with what we often think of as the next one. Here we're healing pieces of the distress at different times.

Me: Would you like to name the truths?

B: Yes!

I'm free to follow my own path.

I can be whoever I want.

I'm agender—I'm not a man or a woman.

No one can tell me how to live my life. I'm a free agent.

I can freely choose not to participate in things that don't fit who I am. I can walk away if need be.

I am FREE!!!!!

Me: Yes, you are!! Congratulations!

B: Thank you.

Me: It's an honor to support you. Is there something else you'd like to look at together today?

B: Not right now, but soon. Is that okay?

Me: Certainly—it's up to you. See you again soon.

Living in a Female Body
April 21, 2023

Me: Hi, Bat-teen—it's Kirin. Would you like to connect again?

Bat-teen: Oh, yes! I have a lot to share with you. I got out some more kohlrabis, and they seemed to be coming faster and bigger. It was overwhelming! So I stopped.

Me: And do you feel as though there's more to get out?

B: Yes.

Me: How about we find a different way to get that stuff out?

B: That would be great.

Me: It's really up to you how you do it. You released a lot of stuff with the kohlrabis, but you can switch to a different method for what's left or for some of what's left.

B: How about if I open my mind and let it evaporate?

Me: Yes, that's certainly fine.

B: Okay, I'm going to do that now... (It's releasing like steam into the air.) I think it's mostly done now.

Me: You're welcome to let it continue behind the scenes for as long as you like.

B: It can continue behind the scenes, but I don't want to do it more now with you.

Me: That's fine. What *would* you like to do?

B: I don't want to be in a female body...

Me: I understand you feel that way, and I welcome *all* of your feelings and experience. At the same time, I want to share with you that that's the most difficult of all the things to change, at least as far as I know. Some people born in a female body have an operation to have their breasts removed, and some have a hysterectomy, though not to get rid of female body parts for that reason. They do it if there's a disease that makes it important for the body parts to be removed. I hope you won't cause any illness out of a desire to be less female physically. There are other things we can do to help that aren't scary or risky. I have a request that you allow me to stay healthy. Otherwise, we can't do what we're here to do.

B: I hear you. But what else can help?

Me: Do you remember when we were about ten pounds lighter and less curvy?

B: Yes, I liked that a lot.

Me: Me, too. I'd like it if we could get back to that. I'm going to ask Heather (healthcare practitioner) for help with what I'm eating. Maybe she'll have some suggestions about ways to cut back a bit on calories. Also, my feet are feeling better these days, which means I can take longer walks. That'll certainly help.

B: That sounds good. That all sounds healthy. I don't want you to be sick.

Me: Thank you. I'm so glad and grateful we're in alignment about that.

It's fine if you're not ready to talk about this yet, but I'd be deeply grateful if you could call off the war on my body. I *promise* you that we'll keep moving in the direction of helping you feel happier.

B: I have a concern. What if I do that and then I get annihilated?

Me: Please let me know what that concern is about.

B: I'll get absolutely bulldozed by people who have agendas for me. I won't be able to withstand it. It'll crush me.

Me: I know it felt like that in the 1950s and 1960s, but it's 2023 now. I'm here right by your side, and so is Charlie. I promise you that you won't get bulldozed. You're safe. What are you specifically concerned you'll get bulldozed about?

B: Giving up my will to live because of all the pressure. Dying.

Me: I'm deeply sorry you went through that and felt it was a real possibility. And again, I'm very sorry I wasn't right there beside you back then. But *you made it*!!! Yes, you carry some wounds because of it, but you survived, and that's an awesome thing. That means the people who were trying to force you to be someone else *failed*. They failed at changing you, and do you know the reason?

B: No.

Me: You're very strong and sure of yourself. The cord that connects you to our essence stayed strong. You survived and made it to where we are now. Great job!

B: Thanks, but I don't feel so great.

Me: I need to take a break. I'll be back soon to resume our conversation. I love you!!!! (hug)

I felt bad having to break off at that point, but the attention required for this type of parts work, combined with insufficient sleep, caused me to suddenly lose focus.

Retrieval and Taking Stock
April 22, 2023

Me: Hi, Bat-teen. It's Kirin. Would you like to connect again?

Bat-teen: Oh yes. I really need your help.

Me: I'm here. How can I help?

B: I don't know how to recapture my will to live. I felt so hopeless during that time that I really thought I was going to die, and I even *wanted* to die at times.

Me: I'm so sorry you had to go through that without support. I know it was really awful, and I understand that wanting to die was an expression of how much pain you were in.

B: Thank you.

Me: I know this probably sounds hard to believe, but all of this can be healed. I know of ways to help you heal. Would you be willing to take a tiny step in that direction? Actually, *another* step? You've already taken quite a few steps.

B: I'd like to keep going if you'll help me.

Me: Yes, of course—it would be my honor. I'm right here. If it feels okay, please tell me what would have helped you feel more hopeful back then?

B: Having someone who cared about what I was going through.

Me: What would they have done to let you know they cared?

B: Given me a safe place to talk about my fears. I was all alone with my fears.

Me: Would it help to rewrite that scene with a caring person added in? Or would you rather leave that scene and travel to a safer place and time?

Giving Bat-teen options feels very important. It was constantly told what to do in the past, and saying no wasn't an option.

B: I want to leave RIGHT NOW. I never want to see those people again!!!

Me: I can help you leave right now. Where would you like to go?

B: I want to be with you—where you are now.

Me: Let's go!

Bat-teen traveled in time and space to 2023 in Oro Valley. In an earlier dialogue, it seemed as though Bat-teen was already in 2023, but repeating the retrieval step as needed is fine.

B: Wow, it's so different here! It's so dry!!

Me: Yes, it feels very different—dry and spacious. This is your home now, for as long as you want to be here. And it's fine if you ever want to go somewhere else. You're free to live wherever and however you want.

B: Freedom—what a concept!

Me: Yes, I know. So different from our childhood environment…

B: Yes!

Me: So, do you have a sense of what would help now?

B: Let me get used to this place. Where can I live?

Me: The whole place is your home—and if you want to be near me, this room is my office. I spend a lot of time here. You can be on the bed with a bunch of animal friends if you want, or sit in the rocking chair, or anywhere else you want. You're free!!!

B: I don't feel quite as dreary as I did before. Everything feels better for having some choice in what I do and what happens to me.

Me: That's great! I was thinking about things yesterday and thought maybe a big part of your distress had to do with a lack of choice—about the kind of body you had, how you felt about it, and a lot of other things. We didn't grow up in a home where we were allowed to choose much of anything, but that's all changed now.

B: I really need to be able to choose.

Me: And I want to support you 100 percent in that. How can I support you?

B: Don't make me do *anything*.

Me: That's fine—I'll ask rather than telling.

B: That's good.

Me: What else can I do?

B: I told you before about stuff like not making me dress up and not being a doormat.

Me: Yes, I'm fine with those things, and I appreciate your letting me know how important they are. What else can I do?

B: I don't know. I still feel awful, though… a little bit better, but still awful.

Me: May I share a few thoughts I've had about the situation?

B: Sure.

Me: I think this may be confusing or hard to fully tackle because it's a bunch of intertwined concerns:

1. Lack of choice about the sex of our body as well as many other things

2. Not feeling at home in a female body—periods, breasts, reproductive capacity, and more

3. Body invasion—being poked and prodded as well as intrusive comments about the size and shape of our body

4. A sense of isolation resulting from profound lack of support as a child

5. Gender indoctrination in general

Does that fit at all with your understanding of what's going on with you?

This is an attempt to identify specific threads in the huge knot of puberty trauma. Before working with IFS therapist and consultant Sundaura Lithman (first mentioned on page 4), I only experienced it as a single enormous knot. By the time of this dialogue, working with Bat-teen had helped me gain an understanding of some of its components. It felt important to share the emerging big picture with Bat-teen as well as invite its input. After all, this is a collaboration.

B: Something to add: Being treated in humiliating ways because of not fitting in. It wasn't just about not having support at home—it was also about feeling like a pariah out in the world and being bullied.

Me: Thank you. I've added that to the list. Anything else? We don't have to make a complete list now, either—we can add to it later.

B: That's all for now.

Me: And have we chipped away at any of them so far?

B: #5 for sure (gender indoctrination in general)—I understand now that gender indoctrination is going on outside of us and doesn't have to have anything to do with us. You've been good at keeping that stuff out. The biggest things were by making sure you'd never get pregnant and by choosing to be with someone who isn't trying to force us into a gendered mold.

Me: I'm glad you sense some forward movement on that one. Have we chipped away at any others at all?

B: Hmmm... let me look at the list... #4 some (isolation about not having any support)... because I know you're here to support me, and so is Charlie. I finally have a safe place to live.

Me: That's great—I'm so glad you know that. And there are many other people in the world who support what we're about. We don't necessarily know them personally, but we know about them and can read their words, like Jennifer Finney Boylan, whose story is inspiring. If you want, I can find more stories like that. And Sundaura Lithman (IFS consultant and therapist)—she definitely understands and is available for support whenever we want to talk with her.

B: Oh yeah—I like her. She understands.

Me: Yes, and she's part of a community of people who understand. There are *lots* of people out there who do, and as for the others, it's their loss. It has nothing to do with us. It's just their limited worldview, and we can't do anything about that, so we'd best not lose a lot of energy over it.*

B: Okay—I get it. This is all really helpful. Thank you.

Me: You're welcome! This is about boundaries—something we didn't have or learn about growing up. Boundaries are about honoring who *we* are and also letting others be different. As long as they don't have power over us, we can just walk away.

---

*This isn't in any way meant to discount the value of social activism.

And if they try to have power over us, we can speak up and tell them to stop. I'm here to do that.

B: This all sounds good. Boundaries—I'd like to learn more about that over time.

Me: Sounds good. I'm starting to have a bit of a hard time staying focused. Can we talk again tomorrow?

B: Yes, that's fine. Thank you for your help and support. See you soon!

Me: Please make yourself at home.

Asking the Right Question
April 23, 2023

Me: Hi, Bat-teen! Would you like to connect for a little while?

Bat-teen: Oh yes! I love that you're checking in with me regularly. It's helping a LOT!!

Me: I'm so glad! It's a pleasure to connect with you and an honor to support you. What would you like to focus on today?

B: Not liking being in a female body.

Me: Okay, great. Is there anything that's helped so far?

B: Not getting periods anymore was a MIRACLE!!!!! And I liked what you said about losing a little weight and not being so curvy. Let's do that.

Me: Do you have a sense of what would help with that?

B: I get really agitated sometimes because I feel like a big bundle of needs, and food helps me calm down. Maybe if we keep addressing the needs, I won't feel such an urge to eat. I think food was my main way to let off stress when I was living with those people.

Me: Yes, that makes perfect sense. There weren't many options besides food, solitude, and waiting for the future to arrive.

B: Yeah, that sounds about right. And nature and Boomer—both of those helped a lot.

Me: And what would help now?

B: I know you're working on simplifying your days so you're not just a work machine. Everything you do to create more calming time will help. Watching squirrels, reading, sitting and listening to music, watching movies, even puttering—anything that helps me understand I don't have to be focused and goal-oriented. I don't want to work so hard. I don't think most of the other parts do either.

Me: Thanks for that information. I'll pay more attention to that going forward. Anything else?

B: Well, weighing less would be nice, but I still have a female body, and I kind of wish I didn't. But I definitely don't wish I had a man's body instead!!! I wish I had a neutral body.

Me: I understand that completely. Unfortunately, that's not really an option for adult humans except for a few who have health problems because of it. Let's not invite any health problems, okay?

B: Okay. I don't want that either. What are the other options?

Me: We can envision a future in which there are more options for genders and body types. And not everyone has a body meant to play a role in reproduction. However, bodies usually change before people really know who they are.

What do you wish had happened in the few years before puberty?

B: I wish someone had *known* me enough to know that I didn't like or want the changes that were coming. I wish I'd had someone who really knew me and cared about me who could have helped me feel taken care of. Knowing how times have changed since then, I wish someone had offered me puberty blockers so I could have had some time to think about things before the changes happened. But, hmmm… what I really needed most was support. I probably could have gone through *anything* with good enough support.

Me: That's very insightful. Do you mean maybe it's not so much about the physical changes you went through as the lack of emotional support during that whole time?

B: Yes, that's it!!

Me: That's very different from the body thing.

B: Yes, I guess it is. It's all been really tangled together till now.

The process of untangling the knot seems to happen organically when I ask the right questions. So much of this process is about listening well, setting aside my ideas about how things should proceed, and asking the right questions…

Me: One of the big ways that Sunny (Sundaura Lithman) has helped and supported us is to explain that it's easier to address concerns and heal if they're untangled. We'll do more of this soon. Sound good?

B: Yes, I'm liking this a LOT! Thank you!!

Me: And thank YOU!!!

Rewriting an Old Trauma
April 24, 2023

Me: Hi, Bat-teen. It's me—Kirin. Would you like to talk?

Bat-teen: Yes, I'd love to. It's great to be able to talk with you so often. I never had that before.

Me: I know, and I'm sorry about that. I'm here now.

B: Thank you.

Me: What would you like to talk about today?

B: Support. How can I heal the parts of me that longed for support and didn't get it?

Me: Let me check with you about something. IFS says that parts in pain are stuck in the past and that they think the bad stuff is still happening. But you don't seem stuck in the past. You seem here now with me—but it sounds as though you remember—or have a part who remembers—not being helped or supported, and *that's* what needs healing. Does any of that fit with your experience?

B: I don't feel stuck in the past—I really get that I'm here with you now—but I have a part who carries a lot of pain about having had to go through that difficult time alone.

It's so great to be able to use parts language with Bat-teen.

Me: Would you like to release and heal that pain?

B: Oh, yes!

Me: And would *that part of you* like to do that?

B: Maybe not yet, but eventually.

Me: What needs to happen first? What feels right?

Bat-teen no doubt knows better than I what needs to happen next. These dialogues are powerful demonstrations of the wisdom of parts. So much of my job involves simply getting out of the way while maintaining a supportive, Self-led presence. My parts feel respected when I let them guide the way.

B: The part needs to name what was so hard. It's all tied up in a ball of yucky stuff.

Me: This is a safe place for the part to share anything it wants to. We can witness it and welcome whatever it wants to share.

B: Great. The part says, "It was really hard to grow breasts and have a constant visual image of Mom's breasts, which I REALLY didn't want to see and didn't want to be tricked into seeing regularly. That was REALLY CREEPY."

This is a reference to an event mentioned in Chapter 3—my mother repeatedly calling me into her bedroom right after she got out of the shower and before she put on any clothes.

Me: Does the part want to make a list, or should we focus on each thing as the part names it?

B: Let's deal with each thing it names.

Me: What would have helped the part when Mom first exposed her breasts?

B: It would have helped if someone had stepped in to say, "Stop—that's not appropriate, and you can't do that!" I was too little to speak up about that, and she wouldn't have listened or respected my wishes.

Me: Would you like *me* to step in and tell her?

B: Can you do that? Can you travel back in time?

Me: Yes, certainly. Are you comfortable visualizing that scene with me and rewriting it, or would you rather stay in the present?

It's important to give Bat-teen a choice so it doesn't have to relive any trauma it doesn't want to.

B: No, I want to go back. I want to see you slay her. There were so many times when I didn't have any choice but to go along with her. I want to see someone stand up to her.

Me: Okay, let's do it. Remember—I'm always here to support you.

I visualize the scene of my mother calling me into her bedroom. She's just gotten out of the shower, and she's naked. I (Self) tell her firmly that she tricked me, that I don't want to see her naked, that I'm setting a boundary, and she doesn't have to like it—she just has to respect it. She gets manipulative and talks down to me as though she's speaking to a fragile little girl (a common ploy of hers), and I tell her to stop that right away. I repeat that I'm setting a boundary, and I say that she needs to agree to never again *call me in her room without either being fully dressed or else telling me in advance that she's naked so I can consciously choose whether or not to come in. I'm really firm with her, and I don't give her a chance to pull her shit. I tell her if she won't agree to my terms, I won't come in her room anymore. She finally agrees.*

Me to Bat-teen: How was that?

B: Great—really great! You didn't give her any room to manipulate you. That was great to see.

Me: Yeah, I know her tricks from years and years of exposure to them. I have a zero-tolerance policy with them now. I've really learned how to be assertive over the years, and I've learned what's reasonable to ask or demand and what isn't.

B: I want to learn from you about that. Sounds like some really useful skills.

Me: They are! I'd love to teach you about them and anything else you'd like to learn. I've learned a *lot* over the years!!

B: Great!

Me: So, if it feels right, check back with the part of you that carried pain about that situation with Mom. How's it doing now?

B: Better, for sure. It's powerful to see a bad experience so vividly transformed. Woo-hoo!

Me: Great! Would the part like to unload any burdens or wounds it took on?

B: Well, I notice there's a memory of having to "swallow" a lot of discomfort and stay sort of frozen in place in her room. Now there's a different script—one of firmly setting a boundary with her—but the body discomfort remains.

That's some amazing discernment on Bat-teen's part—and also an echo of my general experience of my life. I've done a huge amount of emotional healing over the years, but much of it doesn't seem to translate into body healing. I've made significant progress around exercise and eating, but a frozen, stuck somatic layer remains.

Me: How about if we release it?

B: Sure—that would be great!

Me: The part can release it to air, earth, fire, water, or anything else. What sounds right?

B: Fire. Let's burn it up!

Me: Let the part who carried pain about that situation with Mom picture whatever scene feels right.

An image comes of an underground pit that's burning, like an opening in a lava tube. The part is kneeling on a really thick insulated pad that's fireproof and heatproof, and throwing up all that discomfort into the pit.

Just let it happen for as long as it wants to. And it's also okay if the scene changes.

I get a sense that the pain being released isn't just about that one recurring situation with my mother.

What else is involved in the body discomfort?

Bat-teen's part: (naming things as they're released)

—Having to submit to Dad's violence

—Siblings treating me in humiliating ways

—Leon (a friend of my father) molesting me

—Shame about not "looking right" in school and afterward

—Having to move away from the small town where I grew up

—Feeling humiliated by Bill's (ex) emotional abuse and by Bruce's (earlier ex) lack of support

—Jean Pierre's (long-ago boyfriend) demeaning treatment

—Stanley's and Len's (long-ago boyfriends) creepy behavior

—Insulting treatment from Mitch (former therapist in the 1980s) and workshop leaders and participants in a training program I was in at the time

—The cheerleaders in high school who made fun of me

—Terry L. (bullying high school classmate)

—X's relentless bullying and hassling and teasing

—Y's violence and lies

Me: It just goes into the earth and is broken down. It has no structure or energy anymore—it's GONE!!! And that means it's out of your body. How brave you are!!

Bat-teen's part: I feel better!!!

Me: Would you like to take in some qualities to fill the space?

Bat-teen's part: Assertiveness. Boundaries. The right to say no.

Me: They're yours!!! Let them fill you up!!!! They're yours forever!

Bat-teen's part: Yay!!

Me: Bat-teen, is there anything else this part needs for now or that you'd like to share or do?

Bat-teen: Just that that was AWESOME!!! And I see how important it is to treat the body, not just the emotions and ideas. Let's do a lot more of this!! It makes everything feel so much more hopeful!!!

Me: I'm here for this process at any time. I *love* doing this with you and am so glad you're available for this deep healing. We'll talk again soon. Love you!

B: (hug)

Resting
April 26, 2023

Me: Hi, Bat-teen! It's me—Kirin. Would you like to connect?

Bat-teen: Yes, I need your help. I was choking earlier. I'm really glad you came to the rescue.

Me: I'm so sorry you went through that. Getting all that yucky stuff out is a big process! Did it help to make it liquid?

We connected briefly outside this dialoguing process, and I suggested possibly envisioning the burdens releasing as a liquid instead of as large, dense kohlrabis.

B: Yes, that helped a LOT. Thank you!

Me: You're welcome. How are you now?

B: Kind of fragile. I've been through a lot.

Me: What do you need? How can I help?

B: I'm not sure. Let me check…

Warmth? I'm seeing a campfire.

A soft, thin blanket around me and a couple of companions to stay close.

Me: Let me go arrange that.

I wrapped plush Henry (leatherback turtle) in lightweight white fabric and put Étoile (blue whale) and Leif (loggerhead sea turtle) next to him with their flippers on his back to comfort him. When I interact with Henry, I automatically seem to switch to he/him pronouns. I don't try to figure it out or be consistent—I just go with whatever is present as long as there's no pushback from any parts of my system.

How are you feeling now?

B: Better, but I'll need some time to heal.

Me: Of course. That makes perfect sense. Is there anything you'd like from me while you're healing, or should I leave you alone? Either one is fine—whatever you need.

B: I just want to rest for now. I'm exhausted.

Me: I understand. Please let me know when you'd like to connect again. I'll be here! I love you!

Healing from an Unburdening
April 27, 2023

I had a distinct feeling at one point that Bat-teen wanted to connect with me in the interim, but I didn't act on it. A few other parts came up, particularly one that strenuously resists having to be on call whenever others need me. (Good thing I never had kids...)

Me: Hi, Bat-teen. I'm here. Sorry for the delay. A couple of parts came up, and I didn't calm them down right away. But I'm here now. How can I help?

Bat-teen: I need to know I can reach you when I need to—when I'm in distress.

Me: Yes, I know. I'm very sorry. I messed up. I'll do my best to be better in the future.

B: Okay, but you need to know how important it is for me to reach you. The worst thing about the early times was not being able to get help when I needed it.

Me: I guess I thought Leif and Étoile could help when I was busy doing other things. Please help me understand—is that not true?

B: They help a lot with general comfort and companionship, but they can't help me work through confusion or get to new healing places.

Me: Thanks for letting me know. I get it. I'll do better.

B: Thanks. So, what I need to know is how to heal from what I've been through. Sometimes even the healing is rough on me, like when I was letting out all that stuff (burdens in the form of kohlrabis and liquids). That was really hard, and it was scary. How can I recover from that?

I thought this was interesting—a part needing to heal from an unburdening—but I just went with what came up and trusted the part.

Me: Maybe just check inside and see what would help. It could be a color or a texture or temperature or just about anything. It could be something you imagine taking inside or something your whole being experiences, like soaking in a healing pool of warm water. Just check and see what comes to you.

B: A garden with beautiful, tender flowers and gentle scents.

Me: Wonderful! So imagine you're there, and do whatever feels right to you.

B: Smelling the smells is healing, and there are butterflies flying around. One of them gives me some nectar to drink. It coats my digestive system with a thick syrup for protection. It's like a healing compress for my digestive system. Feels good.

Me: Great. Just stay with that experience for as long as it feels right to do so.

B: Can I ask you something?

Me: Yes, of course.

B: Why don't you come be here with me?

Me: I'd like to. Give me a minute...

Nice experience—a huge butterfly brushed against me.

B: Now I'd like to go home—back to your room.

Me: Okay. Anything I can do for you?

B: What's next in this healing process?

Me: If it feels right, you can take in any qualities you want to fill the space left by getting rid of all the yucky stuff.

B: I want to take in being with you—support when I need it.

Me: Great! I'm here. Anything else?

B: Freedom to be me.

Me: Great! Anything else?

B: Rest when I want it. I've been through a LOT.

Me: Yes, you have—you definitely have. You can rest whenever you want.

B: That's great.

Me: Anything else you'd like to take in?

B: No—I think that's all, for now at least.

Me: And is there any other kind of support you'd like from me now?

B: Not right now—I just want to know you'll be there when I need you.

Me: I'll be there. I'll do my very best.

B: Thank you.

Me: I love you.

Shame and Indoctrination
April 29, 2023

Me: Hi, Bat-teen. It's Kirin. Just want to check in with you. How are you doing today?

Bat-teen: I'm feeling calmer. That garden was really healing. The energy was so soft there. And it's been good to rest. I need to rest whenever I want to.

Me: I notice the last couple of days, I haven't felt like doing much, and I watched a movie. Is that restful to you?

B: Yes—very. I want to do more of that.

Me: That's great. There isn't a lot that needs doing these days—just some chores and a little work and a few errands—and, of course, supporting you and the other parts however feels right.

B: Great. Let's rest a lot. Lots of movies!!!!

Me: Sounds wonderful! Do you want to talk about feelings today?

B: What do you have in mind?

Me: Well, I mentioned before about when you—I'm pretty sure it was you, anyway—declared war on my body because of the bodily changes that came with puberty. Do you remember we talked about that?

B: Yes, and you said you were suffering a lot. I remember.

Me: Yes, that's right. Are you the part who did that? There's no shame at all—you and my other parts were in an impossible situation with no support, and I don't blame you *at all* for whatever you all did to cope and survive.

B: I feel ashamed.

Me: You have a part who feels shame?

B: Yes, a *lot* of shame. It's awful to know that we did something that's caused a lot of pain and suffering.

Me: Would you like to work together to heal that shame?

B: Oh, yes. I don't want to keep feeling this way. It's awful and embarrassing, and I'm afraid it gets in the way of being close to you.

Me: I *promise* you that I still feel deep caring and love for you. Nothing can change that. You'll always be very precious to me. People and parts do extreme things when they're in great pain. I don't blame you at all for what you did. The important thing is that you survived!! You survived under intolerable conditions so we could be together now. And it's never too late for healing. Let's be partners in that.

B: Okay.

The shame part seems to have stepped back some.

Me: Is there anything I can do or say to help?

B: I just want to heal. I want things to get better.

Me: Great—and they will. Is there anything you'd like me to know about how awful it was back then?

B: Just total isolation. Nowhere to turn to, and no one who *wasn't* trying to force me and my life into a tight box that I didn't want to go into. I'll *never* go into that box. Grrrrr!!!

Me: That's *great*!!! Despite what others said at the time, that's one of your strengths—your refusal to go along with the indoctrination.

B: What's that mean?

Me: The dictionary says indoctrination is "the process of teaching a person or group to accept a set of beliefs uncritically." That means teaching someone to believe a certain way without questioning it or refusing it. That's what happens all the time in our culture around gender and gender roles.

B: Yeah, why didn't anyone talk about it back then?

Me: They were all indoctrinated with those beliefs, so they didn't have the ability to challenge them. Mom and Dad were more open-minded than many other people of that era, but they still subscribed to many of those beliefs. Also, their *ideas* were more enlightened than their *feelings* about the subject.

B: What do you mean?

Me: Mom understood that women are pushed into domestic roles, and she pushed back against that somewhat in her own life, but she didn't understand that she was doing it to me. She said she was afraid I wouldn't fit in, which is why she pushed me toward certain "feminine" things.

B: That's bullshit. I *didn't* fit in. She just kept spouting the same old crap, even though I wasn't buying it.

Me: Some of that *is* bullshit—and her distorted thinking. And some of it came from *her* fears about not fitting in. She was different from many women of her time, but she walked a fine line and only let herself stray so much. Also, she had a very inflated sense of who she was—and who she was in my life. She thought her opinions and beliefs carried a lot more weight with me than they did.

Also, an important part of adolescence is breaking away from one's parents and learning to think independently. You and I had a big head start compared with lots of people, but the fact that we maintained our own values and truths means we survived—and succeeded! We went through a lot of painful stuff, but we made it. We think independently, and we have our own inner compass. That's a HUGE victory!!!!

B: Wow, now that you put it that way, I guess we did. Yay, us!!!

Me: Yes, it's magnificent. So however we did it, we got to this wonderful present time and place.

B: I feel more hopeful now about being able to go forward. Thanks for explaining all that to me.

Me: I'm happy you're feeling better. We can talk anytime and about anything.

B: Great!

Me: So how's that shame part doing now?

B: Better—calmed down a lot. I wish those painful times hadn't happened, but like you said, we learned a lot and came out being independent. I like that inner compass thing.

Me: You've always had great instincts about right and wrong. I'm just sorry I wasn't there to support you earlier. I'm so glad we're connected now.

B: Me, too.

Too Much to Endure

Bat-teen: So, did you want to talk about declaring war on our body?

I find it both wonderful and amusing that Bat-teen asked this question. Bat-teen seems to be tracking our conversation really well.

Me: Only if it feels right and okay and safe to you.

B: Let me check... Well, I definitely don't want you to suffer anymore, but I'm still confused about how not to feel angry about having a female body.

Me: Thanks for your honesty. It's so great to be able to talk with you about every aspect of this. I so appreciate your openness in sharing what's true for you.

B: Thanks.

Me: So, I can say a few things about that. One is that there's a basic piece of wisdom (the serenity prayer) about how we can change certain things in life, and others we can't, and how important it is to know the difference between the two. One of the things that's true of just about every human on the planet is that they're either born in a female body or a male body. That's the form that most animals take when they come into a body, just as sunflowers have bright gold flowers and cactuses have waxy skin. There aren't unlimited choices when we choose to take physical form, and for almost every human, it's either a female body or a male body. Are you with me so far?

It feels like an honor as well as a significant opportunity to share this information with Bat-teen.

B: You mean it's a diminishment of who we are at our core?

Me: Yes, I suppose it is. When we come into human form, we're basically agreeing to certain rules, like having red blood and a nervous system and walking upright. It's all part of a package. And going through puberty—developing into the adult form—is part of that package.

B: I hate it!!!

Me: I know you do. But can I just share a few more things with you about that? I *promise* there'll be plenty of time for us to acknowledge and explore your feelings about all of this…

B: Okay, go ahead.

Me: Well, one thing is that I'm guessing a big part of your distress is that you didn't have any support to go through those changes—and another part was all the YUCK that people *attached* to those changes—like it means you should look and act and feel in certain ways and not other ways.

B: Yes, that's the worst of all. It felt like a death sentence. NO FUCKING WAY was I going to let that shit happen to me!!!

Me: That impulse to resist the indoctrination was a very good and important one.

B: So what are you saying?

Me: If it feels okay, imagine this for a moment: You're born in a female body, but it doesn't mean *anything at all* about how you should behave. In other words, you're completely free to look and feel and live your life however you want. *And* you have really good support to follow your own inner compass. How does that feel?

B: Spacious. No restrictions, no programming, no bullshit. My life is mine—no one else's.

Me: YES!!!!!

B: It feels terrific!!!

Me: I wonder if gender indoctrination and Dad's authoritarianism and Mom and Dad's self-righteousness all got balled together—like you were already denied so much choice and agency, and then puberty was one more thing—one too many things to endure where you had no choice and no support. That's way too much to bear. Something had to give...

B: (weeping) Yes, I couldn't take it anymore. Between Mom's and Dad's craziness and the siblings' craziness and nonstop fighting and threats and noise and aggression, and then puberty, it was way more than I could handle. I cracked.

Me: Absolutely understandable. Mom and Dad put you in an impossible situation. Of course you cracked.

B: (weeping) It was just too much—way too much.

Me: Is it too much to feel it now?

B: It's a lot, but it's not too much. I don't want to carry this around anymore.

Me: And you don't have to. I'm here to support you and help you heal. What do you need now?

B: More rest—this is hard stuff to go back into.

Me: You can rest anytime you want. And I'll be here whenever you want to talk more. I love you.

B: I love you. I'm so grateful for you.

Me: I'm very grateful for you, too.

May 4, 2023

For some reason I don't remember, I started to refer to Bat-teen as Henry at this point and using he/him pronouns. If the part asked for that change, I didn't record it. At any rate, it felt right. Henry the part doesn't particularly resonate with being male—he simply experiences anything not female as a relief.

Henry just needed to rest today. I said I'd check back the following day.

A Vigilant Protector
May 5, 2023

A protector part doesn't want to proceed with the difficult feelings, but Henry wants to be free. It's a bit of a polarization. I ask Henry if it's okay to listen to the protector with compassion for a few minutes with the understanding that it doesn't get to run the show—it's simply the next step in our process. I reassure Henry that I'll be right here by his side no matter what. Henry consents, though he's a little melancholy. He doesn't like being in this limbo state—it's uncomfortable.

Me: Is the reluctant part available to talk with me for a few minutes?

Reluctant part: What do you mean, a few minutes?

Me: Well, really, for as long as you want.

R: Okay, that's better.

My parts don't cut me any slack. I love it.

Me: Thanks. So, I understand that you don't want Henry and me to proceed in working through difficult feelings around puberty. Am I understanding that correctly?

R: Yup, you've got it right.

Me: Would you be willing to share why not?

R: It's all such a fucked-up mess, and it's going to mess him up more to go into it than avoid it.

Me: You're concerned about Henry's well-being. Is that right?

R: Yeah. He's been through so much—I don't want him to have to go through anything more.

Me: That's very thoughtful of you to think about him this way.

R: That's my *job*, man.

Me: And a very honorable job it is.

R: Thanks.

Me: Would it be okay to ask Henry if he *wants* to be protected this way?

R: Henry isn't a good judge of that. He's going to think it's good to power through the pain, but I know better.

Me: When did you start doing this job of protecting Henry from harm and from difficult feelings?

This is a classic IFS question when talking with a protector.

R: I've always been here—ever since the beginning.

Me: Since puberty? The few years before puberty? Early childhood? In utero?

R: Since the thing with the hammer.

When I was seven, my brother, who'd started bullying me not long before, balanced a large hammer on the crossbeam of a swing set and tricked me into taking a seat and swinging. I did, and the hammer fell on my head. I was fortunate not to sustain a brain injury. My mother minimized the event and regularly excused my brother's bullying.

Me: Wow. That was really awful. Thanks for letting me know— and thank you for protecting Henry. What was it like for you to take on that job?

R: Here's this little kid being absolutely pummeled by the people who were supposed to be family. It was hideous to watch such aggression and lack of protection or safety. I had to step in so Henry wouldn't have to live with the trauma so alive and present all the time. Henry's a very sensitive being, you know.

Me: Yes, I know. That's one of Henry's superpowers.

R: *WHAT DO YOU MEAN?!?! THAT'S A WEAKNESS!!!!*

Me: Why do you say that?

R: That's why Henry got picked on so much.

Me: Maybe, but that wasn't Henry's fault. Henry was embodying his gifts in a natural way. The people around him were at fault, not Henry.

My parts really needed to hear this when I was young, but no one had enough access to Self to intervene.

R: Hmmm, that's a curious way to think about it.

Me: What's it like for you to try on that perspective?

R: Weird, but I guess I've always bought into what other people think.

Me: Do you know who I am?

R: You're the grown-up one.

Me: That's right—I'm Kirin. I'm here to help *all* my parts heal and get along more harmoniously. What do *you* need in the way of support?

R: I don't need anything. I'm indestructible.

I SO appreciate why a part of me had to take on this role.

Me: Wow. That's interesting.

R: What, you don't believe me?

Me: I just don't know anyone else who's indestructible. Do you like being that way?

R: Well, I *do* feel kinda stiff.

Me: Would you like to relax a bit?

R: No, no, no—I couldn't do that.

Me: Why not?

R: Who would take care of Henry?

Me: *I* would. I'm here now. I wasn't able to be helpful all those years ago, but I can now. And I'd like to.

R: Who are you again?

Me: I'm the Self/person who's the natural leader of a group of parts that includes Henry and you. I'm here partly to help all of you feel well and heal and thrive.

R: Well, I'll be. I never knew about you before.

Me: I understand, and I'm sorry about that. I didn't know how to show up all those years ago. I didn't have that level of awareness, so I wasn't able to help Henry or you. But I'm here now, and I want to help.

R: *Thank you.* I've been holding up the world alone for a really long time.

Me: I know you have. Thank you—and you don't have to do that anymore. It's too big a job.

R: Yes, it is.

Me: Would it be okay if I take over that job so you don't have to do it anymore?

R: How do I know you'll do it well?

Me: That's a perfectly legitimate concern, and I appreciate your giving so much thought to Henry's well-being. Here's the interesting thing, though—it's not too big of a job for me. I've learned over the years how to support parts well, and Henry and I have developed a really strong bond. I'd be honored to take over the job of supporting him well, if that's okay with you.

R: Let's ask Henry.

I'm impressed that this part respects Henry's right to have a say in this decision.

Me: Sounds like a good idea. Henry, what do you think about this? Would you be okay with a transfer of responsibility so I'm the one to watch over you and help you going forward?

Henry: What will happen to R (the reluctant part)?

I'm also impressed that Henry is concerned about the reluctant part's well-being. It's fairly standard for a protector to have concerns about becoming obsolete if it stops doing its original job, but this is the first time I've encountered an exile having concerns about its protector becoming obsolete.

Me: Let's ask R what it wants. It can choose a different job that isn't so much work—or no work at all! R, what would you like to do instead if Henry agrees to this transfer?

R: I'd like to go to a beach and be very lazy. I want to rest and relax and watch movies and read and not be responsible for anyone or anything. Would that be okay?

Me: Sure! You can go to a beach right now—just imagine it and go there. Take a nap on the warm sand, collect shells—whatever you want. Just rest. You've done a great job of taking care of Henry up until now, but now you can rest. Just rest.

R: Henry, are you sure you're going to be okay?

It's so clear that the reluctant part is looking out for Henry's well-being—and in such a respectful and loving way.

Henry: I think so, but can I let you know if I ever need your help?

R: Yes, of course. Your well-being will always be important to me. I'll be here if you need me.

Henry: Thanks so much—and thanks for all your hard work in the past.

R: You're welcome. It's been an honor.

Me: Yes, I want to echo what Henry said. Thanks for keeping Henry safe all these years.

Me: (to Henry) How was that for you?

H: Good. Let's talk again tomorrow. There's more to explore now.

Me: Sounds good.

Asking an Urgent Part to Step Back
May 7, 2023

Me: Hi, Henry. I'm here. How can I support you today?

Henry: I want to talk about challenges. I have a sense that there's no way to stay current with everything that's going on. It's all too much.

Me: Are you feeling overwhelmed?

H: Yeah. It's a *lot* to look at.

Me: You don't have to go *any* faster than you want to. It's completely up to you what we explore and what we put aside.

H: But you want to get to a place (a cease-fire—in other words, calling off the war on my body), and I'm not ready.

I'm SO impressed by Henry's ability to speak his truth, even if it isn't what another part of me wants to hear.

Me: You're right that I do have a part who feels urgent, but I can ask it to step back for now. I'm sorry you've been feeling pressured. Thank you so much for letting me know. Should I ask it to step back?

H: Yes, please.

Me: Okay, please wait a minute. I'll come back soon...

(To the urgent part) Hi, urgent part. Are you there?

Urgent part: Yes.

Me: I understand your urgency about feeling better and relieving stress, but Henry isn't ready for the cease-fire yet. Would you be okay with stepping back for now?

Urgent part: I'm okay with waiting longer, but I don't want the cease-fire to be forgotten. As long as I have your assurance that it'll come up later, I'm okay with waiting.

Me: I absolutely assure you that we'll get back to it later. You have my word.

Urgent part: Okay, thanks.

Me: Thank you. See ya later.

(to Henry) Okay, Henry. That part stepped back. What would you like to do today?

H: Just be close to you for today…

Me: Okay. I love you.

Later in the day, Henry released some overwhelm into a fire pit, and a T. rex *ate it.*

Then and Now
May 8, 2023

Me: Hi, Henry. Thanks for your patience with the flurry of activity I just dealt with. I'm here now.

Henry: Okay, thanks. Thanks for making time for me.

Me: Of course! You're very, very important to me. I'm very grateful for all the time we've had over the past few weeks to get to know each other, and I'm looking forward to more. How can I support you today?

H: I want to talk about something that's uncomfortable.

Me: I'm here for whatever you'd like.

H: I don't know why those people didn't help me go through the hard times. Can you explain that?

One of the things Henry needs most is to be able to have his questions answered honestly—something that was sorely lacking in my childhood.

Me: Yes, I can, and I appreciate your question. They didn't help because they didn't have access to *their* Self. When people's parts are leading, people can't listen well or offer genuine support because they're run by certain agendas that have nothing to do with being present. Dad was run by work stress and a need for peace and quiet, plus unresolved childhood trauma, and he had a part who got very angry and even violent when he couldn't get what he needed. And Mom was run by stress about her marriage as well as raising five kids and who knows what else. And both of them also carried rigid beliefs about who their kids should be, so they didn't know how to listen when you shared anything about how you were different. Also... we went through puberty nearly sixty years ago, and most people back then didn't even *know* about agender and nonbinary people or about them being a perfectly healthy variation. They never even heard of agender and nonbinary people, which is very different from today.

H: I should have been born today instead of back then. I would have been born into a much more supportive world.

Me: That's probably true in some ways. Today there's something called gender-affirming care. There are people who could have helped you understand what you were going through and could have maybe even given you some options, such as delaying the changes until you had time to understand them and make some conscious choices about them. None of that was available sixty years ago, but we can draw on it today and help you heal from what happened.

H: But you can't change my body or everything I went through, can you?

Me: I can't change the *physical* stuff you went through, such as developing breasts and having periods. But you and I can together help you heal from the emotional wounds of that time—such as not being supported well, not having anyone to talk with or answer your questions, and all the *crap* about how your body type meant you had to live your life in a certain way—all the "shoulds" that have to do with society's expectations for girls and women. All of that is sheer nonsense, and we can help you get to a place of feeling completely free of it. How does that sound?

H: I already feel somewhat better about the "shoulds" because I see how you turned out, and I hear your words about it all being nonsense.

Me: May I tell you something else about that?

H: Sure.

Me: All that crap about how girls and women "should" be was made up by men who want women to serve them and not threaten them. Men in power have spread lies about women being weaker, less intelligent, and even evil. Those lies came from men's desire to hold on to power and fears they had about sharing power. Men have used those lies to keep women from enjoying the same rights as them. There's no validity to any of it. It's all a ploy to use women. It has *nothing* to do with the truth—nothing at all.

H: You mean it's made up to exploit women, right?

Me: Yes, exactly.

H: And we don't have to adhere to it at all?

Me: No, we don't. There are some times when we might behave the way society says we should, like being courteous and gentle, but that isn't because we live in a female body—it's because *all* humans should be able to be courteous and gentle.

H: Oh, I get it! We can *choose* to be courteous and gentle, but we don't *have* to be, right?

Me: Yes, exactly!

H: Talking about this stuff with you is really good and helpful. I've been so confused for so long.

Me: I'm so sorry you've been confused. You received a lot of messed-up messages from Mom and Dad as well as from others. I'm glad that talking with me helps. I'm here to answer whatever questions you have and support you in any way I can.

H: Thank you so much.

Me: Is there any distress from the false messages you'd like to unload?

H: No—I feel pretty good right now.

Me: That's great! Anything else you'd like to talk about or heal or anything else?

H: No—I think I'm good for now. Will you check in with me tomorrow?

Me: Yes, for sure. I love you.

H: I love you, too. Thanks for coming to rescue me.

Me: You're very, very welcome. So glad we're connected now!

My Body

May 10, 2023

Me: What can I do for you today, Henry?

Henry: Can we talk about my body?

Me: Yes, of course.

H: What do you mean "of course"? It's not so obvious to me that you're available to talk about that.

Me: You're very perceptive. I have parts who don't like to talk about my body or focus on it. I'll ask them to step back, okay?

H: Yes, please.

Me: (to all parts who don't want to talk about my body) Can you please step back for now so Henry feels free to say what's on his mind? I promise there'll be time on other days for you to speak if you want to say something.

Multiple parts: Okay, we see that it's Henry's turn right now. But we want a turn some other time.

Me: Yes, of course. That's fine. Thank you. Okay, Henry, this is your time. The other parts have agreed to step back.

H: Thanks. So, what I want to say is that I never wanted to be in a body *at all*, let alone a female body. Why didn't anyone ask me?

Me: That's a great question. Let me ask you something—what's your earliest memory when you were young?

H: I was very young, and I was on the floor, crawling around. There was a dog that pushed its nose into my face, and I hated it. I wanted to go away, but Mom made me stay there and "make nice with the doggie." I hated her, and I hated the dog.

Me: Wow, that sounds very unpleasant. I'm sorry that happened to you, and I can see how that might make you feel you don't like being in a body.

H: Thanks.

Me: May I share something with you? Well, a few things?

H: Yes, of course.

Me: First, we can heal that unpleasant memory. We can do that now, or I can share the other thing first. Which do you prefer?

H: The first thing—heal the memory.

Me: Great. So, there are probably several ways to do that, but the one that's coming to me now is for me or someone else (perhaps a guide) to intervene and let you go away when you wanted to. I or someone else can stop Mom from forcing you to stay with the dog.

H: I LIKE THAT!!! Make her stop!!!!

There's a recurring theme here of Henry wanting someone to intervene and stop my mother's misguided behavior.

Me: Okay, let's picture it together. Let's go back in that scene and give it a better outcome. Okay?

H: Yes, that's great!!

I picture Mom holding little Kirin so Kirin can't get away, and Kirin is squirming and getting angry. I intervene: "Mom—you need to stop NOW!!! You have no right to force Kirin to be miserable. You should be encouraging a sense of agency and choice instead of squelching it." Mom says, "Oh," and I take little Kirin to another room.

H: Wow, that was cool! She's so used to getting her way that she's surprised when someone says no to her, but you're good at it!! That's so great!!!

Me: I'm sorry I couldn't do it back then. It took me a LOT of years to learn how to intervene and set boundaries. But I can sure do it now!!

H: Yes, you can. It's really great to experience you doing that, especially on my behalf. This is just the kind of support I need to keep healing.

Me: Great!! I'll set boundaries with anyone you'd like me to!

H: Can I ask you one other thing for now?

Me: Yes.

H: When can we talk more about my body?

Me: If I'm alert enough, we can talk again after dinner. If I'm not, tomorrow for sure. Is that okay?

H: Sounds good. Please don't wait too long.

Me: Promise!

Anger and More Anger
May 11, 2023

Me: Hi, Henry. I'm here. Would you like to talk now?

Henry: Yes, I would. I want to talk about my body.

Me: That's fine. I'm listening. Please share anything you want to.

H: I don't like it!!!!!

Me: Can you say more? What don't you like?

H: I don't like that it's an invitation for people to comment. I don't like feeling scrutinized ALL THE TIME. It's constant. It's relentless.

Me: How can I best support you around that? What would you like in the way of support?

H: Tell me why that happens.

Me: Well, we live in a sick society that judges people a *lot* by their outward appearance—things like how much they weigh, what shape their body is, what clothes they wear, and how much they conform to fabricated ideals of attractiveness and femininity or masculinity. It's very sick and false, and it's also very hurtful.

H: Why do I have to live in it?

Me: We were born into this culture, and lots of other cultures place the same value on appearance. We'd have to move to some remote part of the world to get away from it.

H: Can we do that???

Me: I certainly understand the desire to do that, but we'd miss out on a lot of things that are great about living in the United States. But that doesn't mean we have to put up with those stupid judgments. We can create a safe space to live where they can't get in.

H: HOW????? Before you, I've always heard that I *had* to listen to those things and even that they were good. Everyone seemed to be telling me the same thing—"You don't measure up" and "You don't have what it takes" and stuff like that. It was really hurtful.

Me: I'm sure it was, and I'm so, so sorry no one was around then to contradict those messages. I'm here now, and I'm here to tell you it's all *nonsense*!!! You can be and do and look however you want, and if anyone else tries to tell you different, we can just tell them *they don't get a vote*. No one else gets to tell you how much to weigh or how to dress or fix your hair or anything else. It's none of their business. None at all!! What do *you* want?

H: I just want to be left alone. Then I won't have to hear other people's opinions.

This is the sentiment of my core protector: I just want people to leave me alone.

Me: I understand completely how you'd feel that way. And... it's kind of like moving to another country—you'd lose out on some really good stuff that comes from connecting with other people.

H: Yeah, like what?

Me: Like friends and support and great conversations and collaborations. I've had some of that in my life and have really enjoyed it, like making music with other people and doing counseling with another therapist, and laughing with Charlie and having really deep witnessing conversations with him. Also the process art groups I co-led with Amy. Those were extraordinary. And coaching conversations with clients. I love those experiences. And hugging and snuggling and holding hands with Charlie. It's very comforting to do those things.

H: Hmmm. I'll think about it.

Me: You don't seem too sure.

H: I don't want to ever have to give up what feels right to me.

Me: And you don't have to! That's the beauty of having boundaries—you can say no to whatever doesn't feel right.

H: Oh, I get it—I can be with others and still say no when I want to. I don't have to go along just because someone wants me to.

Me: Exactly!

H: Well, that sounds better.

Me: You don't have to choose between people/caving and aloneness/freedom. You can have the best of both.

H: How come no one told me this before?

Some form of this question has come up many times in the dialogues. It's so clear how much Henry needed someone to explain to him how the world works and especially how boundaries work—and what a profound difference it makes for him to have that support now.

Me: They were messed up—that's all I can say. Mom and Dad thought they had all the answers, but they weren't really listening to your concerns. They were just spouting old ideas that didn't have anything to do with your needs or feelings. I'm sorry you didn't have support back then. And I suspect it was even more confusing because Mom masqueraded as a feminist. She pretended to be all about women's empowerment while parroting a *lot* of nonsense meant to teach you traditional female roles. I'm so sorry that happened to you. Let's get that out of you whenever you're ready.

H: I'm really angry about it!!

Me: Please share anything you'd like to about that. I'm here.

H: She was so self-righteous and so sure she knew THE ONE RIGHT WAY. It had NOTHING to do with me—nothing at all. I certainly wasn't going to live my life cut from the mold of traditional female roles, and I wasn't even a girl or woman!! She didn't know a thing about me!!!

Me: That's right—she didn't.

H: I want to smash her.

Me: Go right ahead. How would you like to do that?

H: I want to tell her what I think of all of her bullshit.

Me: Please do. I bet it'll feel really good.

H: (to Mom) You lied to me, and you cheated me out of an up-bringing where I could stay true to myself without becoming totally isolated. You only cared about me fitting in—you didn't give a shit if I stayed true to myself. You just groomed me to fit the mold. Well put together. Acceptable. Marriage mate-rial. Putting up with men's power bullshit. FUCK YOU!!!! You didn't give a shit about ME, yet you masqueraded as a con-scious parent. I don't buy it for an instant. You were hell-bent on the agenda of socializing me to fit in. FUCK FITTING IN!!! You can care about that all you want, but don't lay that shit on me. You had no right to try to make me swallow that crap. You don't know me, and you *never* knew me. You just knew your misguided ideas about who and what I should be, and you couldn't understand why I didn't go along with them.

And A HUGE FUCK YOU to your really fucked-up reac-tion to me getting my tubes tied. You didn't give a shit about women's freedom or independence—you just cared about YOUR ideas about what I should do. Well, FUCK YOU. You're so full of shit, it's no wonder I didn't trust you or want to be around you. You brought this on yourself. You deserved every inch of distancing I did, and then some.

I checked in with Henry here about whether it's okay that some of this comes from older parts. Henry says yes—that it's great to know there's a lot of support for his perceptions as well as parts who will go to bat for him. He says it helps him feel less alone. I let him know that many other parts feel the same, and I do as well.

Me: She failed you. It's a prime failure that she advanced *her* agenda and didn't respect who you are.

H: So what do I do now? I don't like being angry all the time.

Me: A *part* of you is angry, right? Or like an angry part, and you also have a softer part or side?

H: I guess that's right. Let's not try to figure it out.

Sometimes Henry is more Self-led than I am...

Me: Okay. Do you have concerns about what would happen if you let go of your anger?

H: She'd swallow me up. She's a devourer.

Me: She *was*—but guess what, she's dead. She's not here anymore, and she can't get to you. She can't reach you. It's 2023 now, and she died in 2019. She's been dead for more than three years.

H: Wait—it's 2023?

Me: Yes, it is—and if you can believe it, I'm seventy-one.

H: NO WAY!!!

Henry (or parts of Henry) seems to need repeated updatings, which is fine.

Me: It's true!!! And I live in Arizona—several thousand miles away from where we grew up. And *nobody* from that time is in my life anymore. Dad's dead, Mom's dead, and the siblings are all across the country, and I don't have any contact with them anymore.

H: Wow, that's quite a change. I guess I need to adjust my thinking.

Me: How does that change things for you?

H: Well, for one thing, I don't think I need to keep fighting. She's not trying to get me to do anything anymore.

Me: That's absolutely true. Sadly, many other people in the world echo her misguided ideas and agendas, but I'm here to make sure those things never happen to us. And remember— I'm really good at setting boundaries and being assertive.

H: Yes, you are. That helps me feel safer.

Me: And I want you to feel safe and confident that you can be exactly who you are. You don't have to change for *anyone*.

H: Wow, that's great!!!!

Me: Is there anything you'd like to unload from those earlier times?

H: Not right now—I'm not sensing anything.

Me: I can help if anything comes up later.

H: Thank you. I think I'm ready to be done for now. Will you check in with me tomorrow?

Me: Yes, I will. I love you!

Sometimes there was a delay in connecting with Henry again. I always tried to at least take a few moments with plush Henry to re-affirm our connection, even if it wasn't a good time for a dialogue.

Still Angry
May 14, 2023

Me: Hi, Henry! I have some time now. Would you like to connect?

Henry: I'm still angry. I understand that it's 2023 now, but I still hate what she did. It's horrible to claim to care about your kids but sacrifice them to the wolves. It's a terrible thing to do.

Me: Yes, that's true. And no reason or excuse makes up for the fact that she did it. It's about the impact, not the stated intent.

H: What do you mean?

Me: It means it had a bad impact on you. Even if she thought she was doing it for a good reason, the result was bad—and *that's* what matters.

H: How could she think she was doing it for a good reason?

Me: She thought we would suffer more if we didn't fit in. That's all she thought—she was trying to help us fit in so we wouldn't hurt so bad. It sounds like a good intention, but it wasn't at all.

H: I'll say—it was traumatic.

Me: She thought she was making a good choice, but it wasn't.

H: No, it wasn't. So what do we do now?

Me: What feels right?

H: I want to feel free again. That's all I know. I don't know how to get there.

Me: Am I right that we've already established the following?

1. You know it's 2023, Mom and Dad are dead, and the siblings are far, far away.

2. We don't have to follow any of those stupid rules. No one is telling *us* how to be.

3. I'm 100 percent in support of your freedom.

H: Let me check… The ideas are clear, but I still carry a lot of feelings about this.

Me: Good distinction. I can help you unload them if you want.

H: Yes, that would be great.

Me: So take a moment to think about how you'd like to unload them. You can give them up to air, water, earth, fire, or anything else.

H: I want them to burn up so they won't just be carried to another place—they'll be *destroyed.*

Me: Great. So allow an image to come of how you want them to burn up. For example, you can put them in a bonfire or a volcano, or you can roast them on a stick, or anything else you can think of.

H: Drop them from a helicopter into a volcano, like the one on the Big Island.

Me: Okay, so imagine that. And release anything you want to release into the volcano.

Henry releases: lack of support, hatred, anger, heat, hurt from lack of support, feelings of being betrayed, being made to feel small about being different and "less than" as though he doesn't "have what it takes," throwing/coughing up more of those disgusting kohlrabi burdens. Henry ejects it all in a huge wad.

Me: Great. Beautiful. And if it feels right, take a minute to think of the qualities you'd like to take in and put in that space inside.

H: Absolute clarity that I get to follow my own path. No one knows better than me who I am or who I should be.

Me: Truth. Absolutely. What else?

H: A sense of peace that comes from releasing the anger and simply knowing what's true for me.

Me: Great. And what else?

H: I want to rest. It's taken a lot of energy to keep up this fight for so long. I just want to rest.

Me: Are you ready to rest now?

H: Yes, please. But let's talk again soon.

Me: Okay, great. I love you.

More to Unload
May 16, 2023

Me: Hi, Henry. Would you like to connect today?

Henry: Yes, please.

Me: I'm here. How can I support you today?

H: I don't feel so good. I feel discouraged.

Me: Any idea what's going on?

H: It all just feels so overwhelming. There are so many huge forces in the world trying to ram this gender stuff down our throats. It seems way too big to try to fight.

Me: It makes sense that you'd feel that way, but here's something amazing—you don't have to fight it. Just don't engage with it. It's as if there's a tug-of-war between the forces that want you to conform to some bullshit feminine standards and parts who think they have to resist those forces or fight them or confront them. There's another option—you can just let go of the rope. Just walk away. You don't have to pay attention to anyone telling you what you should do or how you should be. Just walk away.

H: How do I do that?

Me: By unloading any negative stuff you still carry about it—but you may need to do other stuff first, such as talk about it more, express how you feel, and get support and validation from me.

H: How do I know what's the right next step?

Me: Just check inside. Whatever comes up is the right next step.

That's some of the beauty of IFS—there's no external referent. It's all about asking parts.

H: Okay, I'll do that... (pause)

Me: Is there more to say out loud?

H: No.

Me: Are there more feelings to acknowledge?

H: I don't think so—it all feels kind of stale.

Me: Do you need more acknowledgment from me?

H: No—I know you went through it, too, and you know full well what it was like. I feel your support every day.

Me: Great—I'm so glad to hear that. So check again and see if there's anything else to say out loud or unload.

H: What if I *always* have more stuff to unload?

Me: That's fine.

H: I have more now...

Me: That's fine. How would you like to unload it?

H: A big ball of crap that gets propelled into the volcano.

Me: Propel away—anything you want. And you can say out loud anything you want to unload as you're unloading it, but you don't need to.

H: Just more bullshit—more and more and more and more and more…

Henry fires ball after ball of bullshit into the volcano – with a lot of power and intention.

Me: Wow, you've got a lot of power.

H: Yes, and I'm getting stronger every day and with every bit that I release!!

Me: Great! You can just keep doing that every time you remember bullshit or hear bullshit. You can unload any that you ever took on, and you can make sure none enters you in the future. You don't ever have to get to a point where you declare it finished, but it's okay if you do. Either way, it's completely up to you.

H: I want to try this out on my own and see how it feels. Let's connect again tomorrow.

Me: Sounds good! I love you!!

Cease-Fire
May 18, 2023

Henry was upset with me because I didn't check in with him yesterday. I sent him love but didn't ask if he wanted to connect. I apologized and said I'd do that going forward. We talked about my interest in him helping me write a book if he'd like to. He was very enthusiastic about that. I asked what he'd like to focus on today—healing, the book, or anything else—and he said healing. He asked me to start typing before he shared anything more.

Me: Hi, Henry. Okay, I'm ready. At your service.

Henry: I'd like to talk about the worst things about puberty.

Me: That's fine. What would you like to share?

H: No support, no help, no guidance, no choice, and a LOT of hostility and bullying directed at me.

Even though it seems that we've covered this ground before, I trust Henry's sense of what needs attending to. If there's more to process and heal, I welcome it. As always, my main job is to stay present.

Me: Yes. That must have been awful—all of it.

H: Yes, it was.

Me: How can I support you now?

H: Like I said before, I don't really want to rehash every little detail. It's all starting to get a little boring.

Me: Is it boring for *you*, or is there another part who doesn't want you to go into it more deeply?

H: Let me check… Boring to me. There isn't a lot of "juice" left in the details.

Me: Do you have a sense of the next step in your healing?

H: I *think* we're at the point you've been hoping we'd get to— my decision to declare war on my body.

Me: Check and see—it's fine if that's where we are, and it's also fine if something else wants attention.

H: No, I really think we're there.

A part of me has been very, very eager to get to this point for a while. I'm surprised and grateful that this eager part hasn't repeatedly interrupted the process of getting to know Henry. It's mostly been willing to take a back seat, but it's certainly pleased that Henry has reached this point on his own.

Me: Okay. Do you remember that decision?

H: Yes, clearly. I felt backed into a corner and completely overwhelmed by the situation I was in. I couldn't see any other way to deal with the horrible situation I was in—having an adult female body forced on me against my will.

Me: Yes, that must have been truly awful—horrific.

H: Yes, it was. I think it's maybe not quite as terrible (emotionally charged) as it was back then. Talking about it with you and dismantling pieces of it has helped a LOT.

Me: If it feels useful to think about this question, what's helped the most?

H: Not being alone with it, for one. And having you to explain things to me—specifically why others weren't supportive and also how society works with regard to gender so it's not just about "swallowing the Kool-Aid." And also that almost every human has either a male or female body. It wasn't aimed at me personally. You helped me understand that I would have had to be born in an invertebrate body to get out of having a male or female body.[20]

I don't think I'd like being an invertebrate. I came here with specific things to do, and being in a human body is part of it. In order to escape having a male or female body, I would have had to give up a *lot* of other things. Maybe I'll do that in another lifetime just to enjoy the freedom, but I guess I'll have to find my freedom in other ways for now.

Me: I'm all about us being ourselves and following our path, regardless of what *anyone* thinks!

H: Yes, I know, and that's one of the things that's so great about you.

Me: So glad you feel supported!

H: I think I'm ready to declare a cease-fire.

Me: Feel free to take your time… No rush at all…

H: No, I'm ready. It isn't doing *me* any good anymore, and it isn't doing *you*—or the other parts—any good.

Me: What do you need from me in the way of support?

H: Just give me a few minutes…

I have a sense that Henry is sending a message to my nervous system and all my cells. There's a sense that other parts were like a military force guarding the wall. Henry's in charge of them and is letting them know to stand down. They're concerned that they'll be useless and discarded. Henry looks to me for help.

Me: If it feels right, check and see if they understand that their services aren't needed for *that* anymore, but they can find another job they'd like to do.

H: Okay, I'll check…

I thanked the parts for their decades of service and let them know that the function they performed—resisting gender indoctrination and the fate it dictated—was much more important than being connected with my body at that point. The parts really understood that it was a life-or-death thing and that they kept me/us alive. HUGE appreciation for that!!!! The parts feel acknowledged and better. They're proud of having done such a great job.

Me: Henry—would it be okay if I talk directly to those protector parts, or is it better to communicate through you?

H: I want to be in the middle. I think it's better that way.

Me: That's fine, of course. If it feels right, please assure them that they're important to our inner family, no matter what job they're doing. And ask them if they'd like to take on a different job.

H: Let me ask… This group of parts says they understand that doing their earlier job caused some problems, and they're sorry about that. They understand that it's time for them to find a new job, and they're fine with that. I'll ask what they'd like to do instead…

They're wondering if they can help you heal.

Me: That would be wonderful! How would they like to do that?

H: They say they're good at sending instructions to different body parts. They wonder what you'd like to heal first.

I'm amazed and so grateful for their offer of help in this particular way. Ever since I started dialoguing with parts about gender, I've had it in the back of my mind that after I completed this book, my body and health would be my next frontier. I can definitely use their help!

Me: Wow—big question. How about my genital area since I've been thinking about that today?

I've had a mystery condition for a while that I haven't yet found solid help for.

H: They're asking what you'd like.

Me: Vibrant health! Can they help?

H: Yes, they say you should think about the shift in energy and send positive, encouraging thoughts to that part of your body. Do that for a week and notice the improvement. That's just for starters.

Me: Thanks—that's awesome. I'm so, so appreciative!!

H: They say, "At your service!"

Me: Thanks—that's terrific. Henry, I don't have good focus to continue with this today. Can we check in another day?

H: Yes. Please check in tomorrow.

Me: Okay. Thanks so much for your partnership. I love you!

Taking Stock with Multiple Parts
May 20, 2023

I'm not clear on why I started out this dialogue checking in with my parts as a whole instead of just Henry.

Me: Hello, parts. Would anyone like to talk with me today about being in a female body or anything else?

Parts: We don't want to talk about anything. We're angry and grumpy.

Me: Sorry you're feeling distress. Anything you'd like to share about that?

P: We can keep going around and around about this topic of being in a female body, but the fact remains that WE JUST HAVE TO LIVE WITH IT, and we don't like it!!!

Me: I hear you loud and clear. And however you're feeling is fine. I'm not here to change it at all. I'd like to understand a little better what it's like for you, though. What don't you like about it?

P: The fleshiness of it—all cushy and snuggly, as if we're designed for our body to be a comfort to others—sexually, parentally, even visually. We're not some fucking decoration!! That's not what we're here for!!!

Me: I understand completely. And we've received a LOT of messages and pressure over the years to be decorative, compliant, and comforting—even pampering—to others, at our own expense. No one ever asked what would nourish *us*.

P: Yes, exactly. And now it's time for US. It's OUR turn now, but the pressures remain.

Me: If it feels okay, can you say more about the pressures?

P: Every time we see women displaying themselves in public with skimpy clothes, it reinforces the message that women are supposed to be sexual objects. We don't *want* to be sexual objects. We don't want other people to have a say in that.

Me: They *don't* have a say in that. No one gets to define us or say what we "should" be doing—about that or anything else.

P: Okay, that's really good to know.

Me: Would it help to review what's better about life now and what's still really troubling?

P: Yes—that would be useful.

Me: Which would you like to start with?

P: Both. Make two lists.

Better:

— Boundaries with Charlie

— Living in a safe home without gender poisoning

— Understanding that we don't have to live by other people's values

— No periods

— No kids

— No evil Aunt Ellie (My mother's sister, who was a generally nasty person, once gave me a fancy manicure set and punished me for not using it.)

— Mom is gone

— Great tools for comforting and empathizing with parts

— Understanding about gender oppression—it's a sick system, not just a personal experience

— I can wear anything I want—gender-neutral clothes

— Name change—a gender-free name and a name not tied to family

— Language around gender and the distinction between body parts and gender

— Understanding that *many* other people are also agender/nonbinary. We're not alone, and we don't have to be confused or isolated anymore.

— Much better communication tools around boundaries and "no thanks" and "not for me"

— Understanding that having a gendered body comes with the territory of being human. We wouldn't want to trade being human for *anything*.

Still Really Troubling:

— Body issues related to menopause—we thought we were done with this!!! A part says, "Why can't I just ignore it?"

— Breasts—a constant reminder of Mom's intrusiveness, narcissism, and lack of ability to understand the effect of her behavior on me. A part says, "It turns my stomach."

— Super-sick culture around sex and gender—the patriarchy in all its permutations

Me: Wow, thanks—this is a great list! Very helpful!

P: It's helpful to us, too—it helps to see how much progress has been made and also shines a light on what to focus on with Sunny Lithman (IFS consultant and therapist) on our next call.

Me: Great! Anything else you'd like to share for today?

P: Do you think we'll get help for this? The good stuff is a *lot* better, but the bad stuff is still really bad.

Me: I have some wonderful guides who have shared that there's a way to live with all of this more peacefully than we are now. I'm going to keep taking the next steps to getting to that more peaceful place. You have my word!

P: Thanks!! It really helps to be able to talk with you about this.

Me: Please let me know any time you want to talk. I want to support you really well.

P: Thank you!

Connecting with an Angry Part
May 25, 2023

I checked in with my parts and got a sense that they're angry about me having to live in a female body. Henry offered to be the go-between.

Henry: Get the angry one to talk. Let's start there.

Me: Okay, thanks. Is the angry one willing to step forward and share anything with me?

Angry part: Whaddya want?

Me: I'd love to get to know you a bit and find out what you're angry about. Would that be okay?

A: No. I just want to be angry. Leave me alone.

Me: Is that what you really want? I don't imagine it's very fun to be angry and alone.

A: Hey, I've been doing this forever. No need to change now.

Me: Certainly there's no need to change if you're enjoying things the way they are. But if you're not, we can put our heads together and see if there's a way to change things so you enjoy life more.

A: Don't give me that crap. There's no way to change what I'm angry about.

Me: And what is that? What are you angry about?

A: Don't play stupid. You know full well what I'm angry about.

Me: Let me guess—having an adult female body?

A: Bingo.

Me: Is there anything you'd like to share about why you're so angry about that?

A: Nobody asked me if this is what I wanted. I hate all this evidence that my body is designed for *making babies*. I don't *want* to make babies. I NEVER, EVER wanted to make babies. I'd rather die than grow a baby in my body *or* raise a baby. What a horrible, thankless task!*

Me: Who told you that you had to make babies?

A: It was always just expected—all those messages about growing up and being a mom, all that crap about practicing on dolls. It's so fucking disgusting. No one shoves that crap down the throats of boys and men. It's just because I have a uterus and vagina and breasts. That CONDEMNS me to a miserable, pathetic life. I want NONE of it. I never wanted any of it. Make it stop!!!!!!

---

* Just a reminder that this is one of my parts speaking—not my general stance.

Me: I can help!!! In fact, I can help in LOTS of ways.

A: Oh yeah????

Me: Really!!! Just for starters, how old are you?

A: I'm sixteen, and I'm miserable. I want to crawl in a hole in the ground.

Me: Do you want to tell me about how you're feeling, or would you rather I share a few things that might help?

A: Help, please… I'm desperate!

Me: Do you have any guess as to how old I am now?

A: Sixteen?

Me: Actually, I'm a *lot* older. I'm seventy-one.

A: NO FUCKING WAY!!!!

Me: WAY!!! And I *never* had children. I was never pregnant, and I never had children.

A: What do you mean?!?!? Every woman is supposed to have children.

Me: Who told you that?

A: I guess I just soaked it up from all the messages around me.

Me: Yeah, when we were sixteen, the year was 1967. There were a LOT of limiting ideas about what was possible, and things were just starting to change. Many people assumed there was only one right way to do things, especially for women. But a lot has changed since then, and that's not the only message going around. Today, a lot of women *don't* have children. More women today, though sadly not all, choose for themselves what kind of life they want. And a lot of people born with female body parts no longer identify as women—and in fact I'm one of them! I don't think of myself as a woman. I'm agender—neither a woman nor a man. What do you think of all that?

A: This is really wild! It never occurred to me that I had any choice in the matter, so I just figured I'd be angry—furious, in fact—forever. If I get to choose my life, that *does* change things.

Me: What does it change?

A: I don't *ever* want children. And I don't *ever* want all that other crap that people with female body parts are "supposed" to want.

Me: Let me interject something, please. You aren't "supposed" to be anyone but your own wonderful self. Other people may *say* you're supposed to be or do certain things, but that's just their ideas. You don't have to follow them *at all*.

A: Wow, that's *such* a relief!!!!

Me: And I'm here to support you in every way I can. You don't have to be alone with these feelings and frustrations anymore, and we can even heal them!!

A: NO WAY!!!

Me: WAY!!! Would it be okay with you if we met again sometime? I'd love to get to know you more and find out how best to support you.

A: Yes, that would be great. I've been so alone with this stuff forever. I'm tired of carrying the huge burden of it. It's too much.

Me: I agree. You don't have to do it anymore. I'll be here to support you, and we'll see about you unloading the burdens you've carried.

A: Thanks so much! How soon? I need a lot of support.

Me: Tomorrow sound good?

A: Yes, that'd be great. Thanks.

Me: See you soon!

Updating the Angry Part
May 26, 2023

Me: Hi there! Would you like to spend some time together now?

The angry part is crying when I check in with it.

It's okay to feel whatever you're feeling. You've been alone with this for a very long time. I'm here now.

Angry part: I'm overwhelmed to think I don't have to just suffer in silence.

Me: No—you absolutely don't. You can get the help you need.

A: I'm SO relieved.

Me: How can I help you today? What would help?

A: Let me think about it for a minute… Tell me more comforting stuff. Tell me it won't always hurt so bad.

Me: I *promise* you that getting support will help you feel better. I can listen to anything you want to share, and I can help you discard the lies and take in the truth about all the freedom you have in your life. There's a *lot* I can help with. Just check inside and see what might make a difference *today*.

A: There's a song that seems to be stuck in my head that haunts me. "To know, know, know you is to love, love, love you. Just to see you smile makes my life worthwhile." What is that *crap*???

Me: It's crap—pure and simple. It's total bullshit indoctrination about women's lives only having meaning because of the man they're attached to. Very unfortunately, we live in a society that's been set up this way *by and for men*. They *want* women to buy these messages so women will keep serving them. They're *using* women. But that doesn't *at all* mean that every woman or person living in a female body has to go along with it or participate in it. Each person can choose. Sadly, so many people absorb these messages, and they end up going along with the crap. But the important thing to really take in is this: *We don't have to do it. We have choice. We get to choose.*

A: Why didn't anyone ever tell me this?

Me: Because they were brainwashed, too. It's a huge, sick system that has taken over societies around the world. It's like an illness that keeps spreading—like a virus. It's called the patriarchy. I'm so very sorry you were exposed to it and that I didn't know how to protect you from it long ago.

A: Thanks. It's really been awful. I thought I had to just put up with it, but something really strong inside me always said NO NO NO!!!!

Me: The part of you that always said NO NO NO is very wise. That's your truth. You can trust it!!!

A: Wow, that makes me feel better. But is there a place for me in the world if I don't go along with this patriarchy thing and don't do what other people think I should do?

Me: Yes, absolutely. Two things about that:

1. Mom gave us the message that there wouldn't be a place for us in the world if we broke the rules. That was *her* fear

that kept *her* in line. It's part of how *she* was brainwashed. She thought it was better to go along than be alone, and the reason is because she desperately needed validation from others. But we don't! We just need *someone* to validate our truths. You didn't have validation back then, but I'm here now.

2. Do you know anything about my life now? I live with a really wonderful person named Charlie who *isn't* brainwashed. He's really loving and supportive, and he doesn't subscribe to patriarchal values. So, I'm *not* alone. It didn't turn out the way Mom predicted— *at all*!!

A: Wow, let me take that in. Do you mean you followed that NO NO NO sense, and everything turned out good?

Me: YES!!!!!! I'm super happy, and I don't feel subjugated at all. I live by my truths, and Charlie is welcoming and supportive.

A: Is Charlie a man?

Me: He was born in a male body, but he's agender, too.

A: Does Charlie have kids?

Me: Yes, Charlie has three adult kids. He was married once before, and they had kids together. He got married very young.

A: Did she *want* the kids?

Me: As far as I know, she did. Or else she did what was expected of her without questioning whether it was right for her.

A: I can't believe anyone actually chooses that path.

Me: I understand. But here's something interesting about the world: things that feel right to some people feel completely wrong to others. And it's not just about being brainwashed. Some people born in a female body feel a very intense desire to have children, and some feel a very intense desire *not* to have children. The same is true of people born in a male body. People are also different in zillions of other ways.

A: I just can't believe anyone would choose that.

Me: I understand. But I also do my best to be respectful of everyone, even if they're very different from me. It's not always easy to do that, but it's my goal.

So, do you have a sense of what would help you at this point? Some ideas are:

— tell me more about your anger and/or how I can support you

— get some or all of that anger out of your body

— come into present time, either here with me or to another place of your choosing

There are probably some other possibilities as well that I'm just not thinking of right now.

A: I think I'm done for today. Will you come back tomorrow? I think I'll have a lot more to share by then.

Me: Yes, absolutely. See you tomorrow!

A: Bye for now. Thanks for coming to be with me. It helps.

Male and Female Bodies
May 27, 2023

Me: Hi, angry part! Would you like to connect today.

Angry part: Oh, yes, please!! I have a lot on my mind.

Me: Please share anything you want to share.

A: Why do people have different bodies? I don't understand that at all.

Me: Do you mean male and female bodies?

A: Yes. What's the purpose?

Me: It has to do with the way many kinds of animals reproduce, or make more of their kind. It's how cells come together and grow into new animals. Humans are animals—just like whales and lions and squirrels. It's just how things are set up and how they work.

A: I don't like it one bit.

Me: Please tell me why not, if you want to.

A: Why does it have to be that way?

Me: That's just how things work for lots of animals, especially complex intelligent animals. Animals need a way to make more of their kind. Otherwise, they'd die out as soon as the first generation died. It's part of the package deal of being born in a human body, with very few exceptions.

A: What do you mean, with very few exceptions?

Me: A small percentage of people are born intersex, which means they have a combination of male and female biological traits. Life often isn't easy for those people. Sometimes doctors use surgery and hormones to force them to just be one biological sex. Others don't have much (or any) support to be different.

A: Why do we have to be one or the other?

Me: I think I understand your frustration, but sometimes there isn't a better answer than "That's just the way it is." But that doesn't mean you have to put up with all the crap that comes with it.

A: I'm really trying to get at what hurts. Why didn't anyone ask me what kind of body I wanted?

Me: I want to be really respectful of your frustration… and I also want to share that in my belief system, someone *did* ask. Or at least we chose what kind of body to be born in.

A: *WHAAAAAAAAAAAAT???? Are you out of your mind?????*

Me: Maybe I am, and please feel free to tell me to shut up if you want. Maybe the soul that you and I and Henry and other parts belong to chose a female body for a good reason. Maybe it wasn't a mistake.

A: I'm not following you.

Me: Well, I believe we come into each lifetime to learn and grow and heal. And maybe one of the things we chose to learn about in this lifetime was gender, and maybe another one was how to heal a body that carries a lot of distress from not feeling like the right home.

A: I don't buy it for a minute. I don't think anyone would choose such a hard task. It seems impossible to heal.

Me: Is this still the angry part talking, or has another part stepped in?

A skeptical part has stepped in.

Skeptical part: Yeah, I'm a big doubter. I don't buy all that New Age stuff about everything having a purpose.

Me: Thanks for sharing that. Whatever is true for you is fine and welcome. But I'm wondering, would you be willing to step aside just for now so I can get back to supporting the angry part? It seems to be in a lot of pain.

S: Yes, that's fine. I just wanted to register my skepticism.

Me: Thanks for letting me know and also for stepping aside.

Angry part, are you still there?

Angry part: I just want to cry. I feel hopeless. I'll never get what I want.

Me: And what is that?

A: I want to be free! I want to fly! I don't want to care about what anyone else thinks!

Me: Would you like to come into the present, where people are freer to do whatever they want?

A: Oh yes!!!

Me: Where do you want to come? You can come to a nature place or my room or anywhere else.

A: A mountaintop. I want to be above people. I don't want to be part of them. I don't want them to affect me.

Me: That's fine if that's what you want—but keep in mind that you can come into the present *anywhere* and not let people's thoughts, feelings, or opinions affect you. It's a matter of building up your inner boundaries, and I can help you with that.

A: Really? Promise?

Me: Yes, absolutely! I'm really good at that.

A: Okay. Can I come be with you?

Me: Yes, I'd be delighted. Do you feel ready to leave 1967?

A: God, yes. More than ready!

I see a huge bird carrying the angry part into 2023.

A: Wow, this is great!!! Goodbye, 1967, and good riddance!!!

Me: Okay, you're here now. Welcome!

A: Thanks! Where are we?

Me: Oro Valley, Arizona—Charlie's and my home.

A: There aren't any other people here.

Me: That's right! Just us!! No one to spew crap from the patriarchy. You're free of that here!!

A: I like it!!

Me: By the way, does the name "Angry Part" still feel right to you?

A: No, I want to be called "Choosing Part." I want free choice more than anything!!

Me: Great—it's yours. That's one of your gifts.

Choosing part: What do you mean?

Me: Sometimes things feel bad *not* because they're bad but rather because we want them very intensely and don't yet have them, and that hurts. But your strong desire for freedom is a great gift, and I feel confident that you'll feel that more as you get more support for it. As the saying goes, "You've come to the right place."

C: Thanks! I'm feeling more excited about the future now.

Me: Terrific!! Hey, I need to go exercise before dinner. Can we meet again soon?

C: Yes. Tomorrow, please—okay? I have so many questions…

Me: Tomorrow it is! See you then. So glad you're here!

A Means to an End
June 1, 2023

Me: Hi, Choosing Part. Are you there? I'd love to talk with you if you are.

Choosing part: Where the hell have you been?

Me: Sooooo sorry. I've been sick. This is the first day I've felt well enough to connect with you. I'm really sorry to have kept you waiting so long.

C: Don't you know how much pain I'm in?

Me: I do, and I'll do my very best to connect with you whenever I can. I see that I need to make more spacious time to connect with you—not just when I have a brief window.

C: Yes—I really need that.

Me: I'll make every effort to make more time for you. How can I support you today?

C: Why do I have to deal with this female body?

Some form of this question has come up a lot in working with my parts. Every time we address it, it seems as though another piece of the puzzle is revealed. Even though this dialogue seems to cover much of the same ground as earlier ones, it leads to a significant shift.

Me: I understand that you don't like it, and I'd like to help you find a more peaceful relationship with it. What kind of body would you rather have?

C: A neutral body. That would be heavenly.

Me: It's fine to want that and to think about it, but did you know that hardly anyone has that kind of body? Even if they *appear* to because of their shape or how they dress, inside they're almost always either male or female in terms of their body parts. It comes with the territory of being human for just about everyone.

C: Oh. You mean I'd have to not be human to not have either male or female parts.

Me: Yes, that's accurate.

C: Well, I certainly wouldn't want to miss out on being human. That makes me want to scream even louder!!

Me: How come? However you feel is completely fine, but I'd love to know what being human means to you.

C: It means I can be creative in ways I want to, and I can travel and be in nature and dream and feel. And love. I think I'm starting to understand that I'd miss out on a *lot* if I weren't human. I'd lead a very simple life, but it's all this complexity that excites me.

Me: Yes—all of that is true. So it sounds as though you don't like being in a female body, but you like certain benefits that it brings. You'd get those same benefits in a male body. Would you like that any better?

C: Hell, no! There's a whole lot of *different* toxic stuff that comes with that, and I'd rather be working to take up more space than less.

Me: So, this seems like a big realization. *Being in a female body is a means to an end.* You like the end—just not the means.

C: Yes, I guess that's true. But I don't want to be fighting the means all the time.

Me: That's very wise of you. So let's get you some help with that. Do you have any ideas?

C: No—I just don't want to be in pain anymore, and I don't want anger to cause inflammation. Do you have any ideas?

Me: A few:

    — lose weight and have a less curvy body

    —find a somatic practitioner who can help

— talk with Sunny Lithman about it

— grieve

— talk with guides

C: It ALL sounds good. Let's go there next.

Me: Okay, sounds good. I'll check in with you tomorrow.

Reaffirming Our Partnership
June 2, 2023

Me: Hi, Choosing Part. I'm here to check in with you.

Choosing part: I'm glad you're here. I have something to say. I wouldn't want ANYTHING to get in the way of us doing what we came here to do. I still don't really understand why I have to live in a female body, but that's secondary to being able to be here. I feel that really strongly. Let's figure this out together.

Me: I'd love to! We're partners, and I'm so glad you feel that. I'm here to help and support you in any way I can. And I don't want you to be in pain or to carry wounding. You deserve to be free of all that yucky stuff.

C: Thanks. I want that, too.

Me: How can I support you now? What would help the most?

C: Can you tell me again how you knew you were agender?

Me: Sure. Did I *ever* tell you about that?

C: I don't know if you told me directly. I've overheard a lot of conversations.

Me: The first thing I remember clearly is refusing to go to kindergarten if I had to wear a dress. I must have been really adamant about it because Mom got permission from the school principal for me to wear pants. I must have already objected to being dressed like a girl, and I certainly objected to it later on. There's an old photo of me as a little girl wearing a little girly dress and with a cute little haircut, and I remember years later that Mom took me to get my hair cut, and I HATED the girly way it made me look. None of that ever fit for me. I liked feeling like a tomboy and looking like a tomboy. And I never understood what it felt like to be a woman. That concept never had any meaning for me.

C: And how do you feel now?

Me: The same. How about you? How do you feel inside?

C: Like a rebel. Like a freedom lover. I don't want anyone telling me who I should be.

Me: And do you think that's specifically about gender or about freedom in general?

C: Everything. It's not just about that, but that's one of the biggest ways I've been told who to be, and I wholeheartedly object.

Me: Yay! Me, too!!

C: So we're partners in that, too!

Me: Yes!!

The choosing part feeling like a rebel and a freedom lover no doubt has to do with both gender indoctrination and having grown up in an abusive, authoritarian environment. I have a group of parts I refer to as my "freedom parts" whose needs and well-being I consistently take into account.

———

At some point after this dialogue, it became clear that Henry (and perhaps many of my other parts) wanted to do a big unburdening ritual in real time. It came to me that they wanted me to read aloud a list of burdens they'd been carrying and then burn it. They also wanted me to read aloud a list of qualities they wanted to invite in.

I spent a good amount of time over the summer checking in with my parts and creating lists of burdens to release and qualities to bring in. When the two lists felt complete, I asked Charlie to facilitate and witness the ritual and tend the fire. On August 27, 2023, he created a sacred space by invoking the four directions and then stepped back so he could witness without intruding. I read aloud the list below of burdens to release and then burned it. Then I read the list of qualities I was inviting in.

Burdens Released
— Lack of support and guidance
— Lack of choice—feeling backed into a corner
— Mom's toxic energy—poisoning from her not welcoming me
— Feeling like a freak—like no one else has ever felt this way
— Feeling totally alone with nowhere to turn for help
— Feeling destroyed by the physical changes at puberty
— Feeling hopeless
— Feeling overwhelmed
— The misery of having periods
— Being tricked into seeing Mom naked and no voice or support to make her stop
— Coercion around dressing "feminine" and being "presentable"

— Having toxic messages about being a woman and a mother rammed down my throat

— Having to "swallow" a lot of discomfort and stay frozen

— Being assigned certain roles because of my body parts

— Indoctrination about growing up and getting married and assuming traditional female roles

— Indoctrination about having to be attractive in conventional ways

— Thinking a certain type of body dooms me to a certain kind of life

— Dealing with birth control

— Toxic messages about "you'll get used to it" (i.e., you'll eventually acclimate to the poison we're feeding you)

— LIES, LIES, LIES

— "The bullshit they fed me"

— Hatred

— Anger and heat

— Hurt from lack of support

— Feelings of having been betrayed

— Being made to feel small because I'm different

— Feeling pressured to feel "less than" and that I don't "have what it takes"

— Giving up my will to live because of all the pressure from people who had agendas for me

— Having to withdraw to survive

— Being controlled and smothered

— Holding myself in a tight ball

— Wanting to move and having to suppress the urge

— Protectiveness and helplessness from having been physically abused
— Fear of relaxing and confusion about how to do it
— Gender grooming—being treated like a lump of clay
— Being bullied, scapegoated, coerced, and ruled
— Being treated in humiliating ways because I didn't fit in—at home, at school, in a training program, and more
— Hostility directed at me
— Drama in all its forms
— Sacrificing my needs and preferences for others
— Sacrificing my needs and preferences to survive
— Having to fight for room to live and be
— Having to fight for the right to be me

Qualities Invited In

— I'm a free agent
— Freedom to be exactly who I want to be
— Freedom to do exactly what I want and create my life however I want it to be
— Free choice—the right and freedom to say yes and no
— Freedom to choose not to participate in things that don't fit who I am—I can walk away if I want to
— Freedom to choose to behave however I want, regardless of how it does or doesn't fit in with traditional gender roles
— Freedom to live by my own values
— Freedom to follow my own path and absolute clarity about my right to do so
— I can rest—I don't have to fight all the time

— Support from the Universe
— Support from Kirin/Self
— Support when I need it (trusting that it's available)
— Being welcome in this home
— Confidence that I can be here and feel nourished
— Vibrant resilience
— Vibrant health
— Healing and growing in peace
— Abundant tools to keep growing and healing
— Abundant beauty in all its forms
— Vitality
— Assertiveness
— Healthy boundaries
— Stability
— Strength
— Power
— Purpose
— Intention
— Integrity
— A sense of peace that comes from knowing what's true
for me and honoring it

Ever since this unburdening ritual, my inner system has felt much calmer. When I think about or deal with the female aspects of my body, such as putting on a bra, it still brings up thoughts such as *Not my first choice* and *This is kinda weird.* However, it also affirms that my parts and I have big things to do in this lifetime and are resilient enough to deal with the challenges that come with the territory. My female body is a means to an end—being here to fulfill my purpose—and that's okay.

I've also noticed feeling quite a bit less angry since the ritual. Many years ago, Charlie observed quite accurately that I carried a "fuck you" in my back pocket at all times. I'm still quick to set a boundary when one is encroached on—no doubt a consequence of having been raised in an abusive, authoritarian home—but my parts no longer feel mad at the world. They feel relieved and grateful to be in such a calm place and proud of themselves for everything they've worked through. They also feel strongly connected to me and trust that I'm available to support them in every way. My system feels peaceful with regard to gender, which I couldn't have imagined was possible just a year ago.

CONCLUSION

It's tempting to wrap up this book with a big pronouncement about what gender is and isn't, and a couple of my parts would love that. It would be easy to take that route, but that's not the purpose of this book. It's not about what I or anyone else thinks about gender—it's about bringing Self energy to parts that have been impacted by gender socialization and the gender binary, supporting them well, and following the trail of healing as it unfolds. Parts who carry burdens about these topics need a safe, Self-led place to tell their stories, be witnessed, and unload their burdens. They don't need someone else, inside or out, telling them how to be or what to do.

Without question, we all carry burdens related to gender. We can't escape it living in such a severely gendered society that seems relentless in its efforts to maintain a power imbalance between women and men. In addition, we've all been exposed to gender socialization from the moment we were born—possibly earlier via ultrasound—when someone, likely a medical professional, looked at our genitals and declared, "It's a boy!" or "It's a girl!" At that exact moment, practically everyone's life was steamrolled onto the "boy track" or "girl track," which was reflected in how we were dressed, the toys we were given, the colors in our nursery, the tone of voice used when talking with us, and more. We were also slapped with a huge load of gendered expectations—from society as well as the emotional wounds our caregivers unconsciously passed along to us. Whoever they wanted us to become, the likelihood that they set aside those expectations so we could grow into our full, healthy selves was pretty much zero.

So began a lifetime of gender-based wounding and an accumulation of burdens related to how we were treated and the programming we received. Those burdens compounded as they wove together with our gender-based expectations of others. Thankfully, however, we're not compelled to live with the fallout. By getting curious about our parts and welcoming them—whatever their truths and whatever they want to share—we can help them heal. Doing so helps us grow in Self leadership and step out of the role of being unconscious carriers of the gendered values of the society we live in. Internal Family Systems provides powerful and effective tools for turning the ship around, no matter how long ago it set sail on a hazardous course or how polluted the waters it has navigated up until now.

I want to be absolutely clear that I'm not suggesting everyone would be agender if they healed their parts impacted by gender socialization. I'm not a gender abolitionist, and I have no idea what's right for anyone else. And although I have no internal experience of gender, I don't mean to imply that others' experiences of gender are necessarily or exclusively parts-driven. Who we become when we help our parts unload their burdens is our unique selves, not a cookie-cutter replica of a different template. Human beings are much too complex for facile assumptions, and our identities are likely shaped by far more influences than we can even begin to imagine.

What I *am* advocating is for all people who don't conform to the gender binary—or any other social hierarchy, all of which are used to marginalize and gain power over people—to be completely free to live our lives in peace and enjoy the same rights and freedoms as the dominant groups. And for *all* of us, including those who *do* resonate with some or all of the gender binary, to have the tools to heal any parts who have been negatively impacted by gender messages so we can live more unencumbered and our internal systems can find greater harmony.

IFS therapists and practitioners understand the importance of being Self-led and monitoring our own parts so they don't interfere with our work with clients. The same cautions apply for people who work with their parts independently. Asking parts who have an investment in particular outcomes to step back is a crucial component of the IFS process. When we do, we can bring Self energy to parts and follow their trustworthy lead on the path to healing.

———

Several times I've checked with Henry to make sure it's okay to share his story, which is intensely personal. If he'd said no, I never would have published this book. But Henry is proud to have others know what he's been through and all the healing work he's done. He's also proud of the bond he and I have forged over the past year. He feels inspired to think that his struggles might have a larger purpose and that his healing and truth-telling might be useful to others who seek it for themselves and their clients. He says it doesn't matter so much anymore what he's been through—it only matters that he's free and can help others get free.

ENDNOTES

1 Duane Brayboy, "Two Spirits, One Heart, Five Genders." *Indian Country Today*, 2017, https://ictnews.org/archive/two-spirits-one-heart-five-genders.

2 Daniel Stables, "Asia's Isle of Five Separate Genders," BBC, 2021, https://www.bbc.com/travel/article/20210411-asias-isle-of-five-separate-genders.

3 Shanna Collins, "The Splendor of Gender Non-Conformity in Africa," *Medium*, 2017, https://medium.com/@janelane_62637/the-splendor-of-gender-non-conformity-in-africa-f894ff5706e1.

4 Anna Goldfield, "Five Human Species You May Not Know About," *Sapiens*, 2021, https://www.sapiens.org/archaeology/ancient-human-species/.

5 Rebecca J. Safran, "Speciation: The Origin of New Species," *Nature*, 2012, https://www.nature.com/scitable/knowledge/library/speciation-the-origin-of-new-species-26230527/.

6 "Tiger," IUCN Red List, https://www.iucnredlist.org/species/15955/214862019#taxonomy.

7 Megan Schmidt, "Genomic Study Confirms There's Six Tiger Subspecies Left," *Discover*, 2018, https://www.discovermagazine.com/planet-earth/genomic-study-confirms-theres-six-tiger-subspecies-left.

8 Jean Hiernaux and Michael Banton, "Four Statements on the Race Question," UNESCO Digital Library, 1969, https://unesdoc.unesco.org/ark:/48223/pf0000122962.

9 "Human Skin Color Variation," Smithsonian National Museum of Natural History, https://humanorigins.si.edu/evidence/genetics/human-skin-color-variation.

10 Nina G. Jablonski, "The Evolution of Human Skin Pigmentation Involved the Interactions of Genetic, Environmental, and Cultural Variables," PubMed, US National Library of Medicine, https://www.ncbi.nlm.nih.gov/pmc/articles/PMC8359960/.

11 Nina G. Jablonski, "The Evolution of Skin Color," Penn State, https://www.psu.edu/impact/story/the-evolution-of-skin-color/; Nina Jablonski, "Skin Color Is an Illusion," 2009, TED Talk, https://www.ted.com/talks/nina_jablonski_skin_color_is_an_illusion.

12 David R. Roediger, "Historical Foundations of Race," National Museum of African American History & Culture, https://nmaahc.si.edu/learn/talking-about-race/topics/historical-foundations-race.

13 Daniel Villarreal, "Can Animals Be Gay? Same-Sex Behavior Is Natural," *LGBTQ Nation*, 2023, https://www.lgbtqnation.com/2023/03/can-animals-be-gay-same-sex-behavior-is-natural/.

14 Barry Yeoman, "Same-Sex Behavior Among Animals Isn't New. Science Is Finally Catching Up," National Wildlife Federation, 2023, https://www.nwf.org/Magazines/National-Wildlife/2023/Summer/Conservation/Same-Sex-Behavior-Animals-Science.

15 Ambika Kamath, Julia Monks, Erin Giglio, Max Lambert, and Caitlin McDonough, "Why Is Same-Sex Sexual Behavior So Common in Animals?" *Scientific American*, 2019, https://www.scientificamerican.com/blog/observations/why-is-same-sex-sexual-behavior-so-common-in-animals/.

16 James Owen, "Homosexual Activity Among Animals Stirs Debate," *National Geographic*, 2004, https://www.nationalgeographic.com/science/article/homosexual-animals-debate.

17 Karen A. Anderson, Julie A. Teichroeb, Malcolm S. Ramsay, Iulia Bădescu, Iulia, Sergi López-Torres, and James K. Gibb. "Same-sex sexual behaviour among mammals is widely observed, yet seldomly reported: Evidence from an online expert survey." *PLoS ONE*, 2024. https://doi.org/10.1371/journal.pone.0304885.

18 Rosa Rahimi. "Same-Sex Behavior Among Animals Is Being Underreported, Study Finds." CNN, June 21, 2024. https://www.cnn.com/2024/06/21/science/animal-same-sex-behavior-underreported-scli-intl-scn/index.html.

19 Kelley Dennings, "8 Billion People on Earth Crowding Out Imperiled Animals, Plants," Press release, Center for Biological Diversity, https://biologicaldiversity.org/w/news/press-releases/8-billion-people-on-earth-crowding-out-imperiled-animals-plants-2022-11-15/.

20 "Hermaphrodite," *Vedantu*, https://www.vedantu.com/biology/hermaphrodite; "Hermaphroditism," *Encyclopedia Britannica*, https://www.britannica.com/science/hermaphroditism.

REFERENCES

Anderson, Karen A., Teichroeb, Julie A., Ramsay, Malcolm S., Bădescu, Iulia, López-Torres, Sergi, and Gibb, James K. "Same-sex sexual behaviour among mammals is widely observed, yet seldomly reported: Evidence from an online expert survey." *PLoS ONE* 19(6): e0304885, 2024. https://doi.org/10.1371/journal.pone.0304885.

Bailar, Schuyler. *He/She/They: How We Talk About Gender and Why It Matters.* New York: Hachette Books, 2023.

Brayboy, Duane. "Two Spirits, One Heart, Five Genders." *Indian Country Today*, 2017. https://ictnews.org/archive/two-spirits-one-heart-five-genders.

Chang, Sand. "Embodying IFS with Trans and/or Nonbinary Communities: All Genders Welcome." in *Altogether Us: Integrating the IFS Model with Key Modalities, Communities, and Trends*, ed. Jenna Riemersma (Marietta, GA: Pivotal Press, 2023), 288–314.

Collins, Shanna. "The Splendor of Gender Non-Conformity in Africa," *Medium*, 2017. https://medium.com/@janelane_62637/the-splendor-of-gender-non-conformity-in-africa-f894ff5706e1.

Dennings, Kelley. "8 Billion People on Earth Crowding Out Imperiled Animals, Plants," Press release, Center for Biological Diversity. https://biologicaldiversity.org/w/news/press-releases/8-billion-people-on-earth-crowding-out-imperiled-animals-plants-2022-11-15/.

Fine, Cordelia. *Delusions of Gender: How Our Minds, Society, and Neurosexism Create Difference.* New York: W. W. Norton & Company, Inc., 2010.

Goldfield, Anna. "Five Human Species You May Not Know About," *Sapiens*, 2021. https://www.sapiens.org/archaeology/ancient-human-species/.

"Hermaphrodite," *Vedantu.* https://www.vedantu.com/biology/hermaphrodite.

Hiernaux, Jean, and Michael Banton. "Four Statements on the Race Question," UNESCO Digital Library, 1969. https://unesdoc.unesco.org/ark:/48223/pf0000122962.

"Human Skin Color Variation." Smithsonian National Museum of Natural History. https://humanorigins.si.edu/evidence/genetics/human-skin-color-variation.

Jablonski, Nina G. "The Evolution of Human Skin Pigmentation Involved the Interactions of Genetic, Environmental, and Cultural Variables," PubMed, US National Library of Medicine. https://www.ncbi.nlm.nih.gov/pmc/articles/PMC8359960/.

Jablonski, Nina G. "The Evolution of Skin Color," Penn State. https://www.psu.edu/impact/story/the-evolution-of-skin-color/.

Jablonski, Nina. "Skin Color Is an Illusion," 2009, TED Talk. https://www.ted.com/talks/nina_jablonski_skin_color_is_an_illusion?language=en.

Kamath, Ambika, Julia Monks, Erin Giglio, Max Lambert, and Caitlin McDonough. "Why Is Same-Sex Sexual Behavior So Common in Animals?" *Scientific American*, 2019. https://www.scientificamerican.com/blog/observations/why-is-same-sex-sexual-behavior-so-common-in-animals/.

Kimmel, Michael. *The Gendered Society*, 6th ed. New York: Oxford University Press, 2017.

Lerner, Gerda. *The Creation of Patriarchy.* New York: Oxford University Press, 1986.

Owen, James. "Homosexual Activity Among Animals Stirs Debate," *National Geographic*, 2004. https://www.nationalgeographic.com/science/article/homosexual-animals-debate.

Rahimi, Rosa. "Same-Sex Behavior Among Animals Is Being Underreported, Study Finds." CNN, June 21, 2024. https://www.cnn.com/2024/06/21/science/animal-same-sex-behavior-underreported-scli-intl-scn/index.html.

Roediger, David R. "Historical Foundations of Race," National Museum of African American History & Culture. https://nmaahc.si.edu/learn/talking-about-race/topics/historical-foundations-race.

Safran, Rebecca J. "Speciation: The Origin of New Species," *Nature*, 2012. https://www.nature.com/scitable/knowledge/library/speciation-the-origin-of-new-species-26230527/.

Schmidt, Megan. "Genomic Study Confirms There's Six Tiger Sub-species Left," *Discover*, 2018. https://www.discovermagazine.com/planet-earth/genomic-study-confirms-theres-six-tiger-subspecies-left.

Schrefer, Eliot. *Queer Ducks (and Other Animals): The Natural World of Animal Sexuality.* New York: HarperCollins Publishers, 2022.

Stables, Daniel. "Asia's Isle of Five Separate Genders," BBC, 2021. https://www.bbc.com/travel/article/20210411-asias-isle-of-five-separate-genders.

Sweezy, Martha. *Internal Family Systems Therapy for Shame and Guilt.* New York: The Guilford Press, 2023.

"Tiger." IUCN Red List. https://www.iucnredlist.org/species/15955/214862019#taxonomy.

Villarreal, Daniel. "Can Animals Be Gay? Same-Sex Behavior Is Natural," *LGBTQ Nation*, 2023. https://www.lgbtqnation.com/2023/03/can-animals-be-gay-same-sex-behavior-is-natural/.

Yeoman, Barry. "Same-Sex Behavior Among Animals Isn't New. Science Is Finally Catching Up," National Wildlife Federation, 2023. https://www.nwf.org/Magazines/National-Wildlife/2023/Summer/Conservation/Same-Sex-Behavior-Animals-Science.

ACKNOWLEDGMENTS

To Batman/Bat-teen/Henry for daring to hope that healing was possible and being willing to share so honestly and openly in service of collective healing;

To Boomer, my equine friend and lifeline as a teen, for loyalty, support, and Self energy;

To my father, Lou Silverberg, for being a fierce model of refusal to settle for the status quo;

To Sundaura Lithman for editorial feedback and encouragement as well as insightful and compassionate support to crack the code of my gender-based distress;

To Dick Schwartz for developing the Internal Family Systems model, which has been instrumental in my life since 2007;

To Judith K. Brown for extraordinary anthropology instruction and for planting the seeds of this book by introducing me to the fields of gender studies and cross-cultural analysis;

To Schuyler Baylor, Cordelia Fine, Michael Kimmel, and the many others whose work has helped create a strong collective foundation for understanding gender and gender-based oppression;

To Joel Baum for valuable insights into gender socialization as a form of indoctrination that affects all of us, regardless of gender identity;

To Kim Daniels and Wren Wood for feedback and encouragement;

To Carol McClelland Fields for guidance on marketing for introverts and for helping me stay on track with publishing this book;

To Robert Henry, publishing wizard, for all sorts of help;

And to Charlie, my great love and dearest friend, for editorial feedback and encouragement, for this amazing adventure we're on, for joyous partnership in living free of the gender binary, and for opening my eyes and life to what's possible when two people connected by a red thread finally find each other.

ABOUT THE AUTHOR

Kirin Alolkoy, MA, BCC, LPC, is a Board Certified Coach, Certified Purpose Clarity Coach, Licensed Professional Mental Health Counselor (inactive), and freelance writer who holds master's degrees in integral counseling psychology and anthropology as well as advanced training in the Internal Family Systems (IFS) model. Her human development work blends life and purpose coaching with IFS to explore living true to oneself and shedding familial and cultural expectations around gender and other concerns.

In addition, Kirin has written more than three hundred K–6 nonfiction books and countless reading passages for educational publishers. The materials, which are used to teach elementary students to read, explore high-interest topics at graduated levels of complexity. Kirin is also the author of *Losing and Finding My Father: Seasons of Grief, Healing and Forgiveness* (published under her previous name).

Kirin lives in Tucson, Arizona, with her spouse, an artist and nature photographer. She can be reached at:

Website: kirinalolkoy.com

Facebook: tinyurl.com/ju5vte3w

www.ingramcontent.com/pod-product-compliance
Lightning Source LLC
Chambersburg PA
CBHW051723020426
42333CB00014B/1116